Louis Wain's CATS

Chris Beetles

with contributions from
Rodney Dale and David Wootton
Foreword by Benedict Cumberbatch

CANONGATE

For Lesley Anne Ivory, the greatest living cat artist, who would understand.
— Chris Beetles 2011

This edition published in Great Britain, the USA and Canada in 2021 by Canongate Books Ltd,
14 High Street, Edinburgh EH1 1TE and Chris Beetles Ltd

First published in Great Britain in 2011 by Worth Press Ltd and Chris Beetles Ltd

Distributed in the USA by Publishers Group West and in Canada by Publishers Group Canada

canongate.co.uk

Copyright © Chris Beetles, 2011
Foreword copyright © Benedict Cumberbatch, 2021

The right of Chris Beetles to be identified as the
author of this work has been asserted by him in accordance
with the Copyright, Designs and Patents Act 1988

Extract from *The Electrical Life of Louis Wain* used courtesy of StudioCanal

Every effort has been made to trace copyright holders and obtain their permission for the use of copyright material. The publisher apologises for any errors or omissions and would be grateful if notified of any corrections that should be incorporated in future reprints or editions of this book.

British Library Cataloguing-in-Publication Data
A catalogue record for this book is available on
request from the British Library

ISBN 978 1 83885 470 6

Design and layout: Arati Devasher, aratidevasher.com

Printed and bound in Italy by LEGO S.p.A.

Pages 1: THOSE WITH FEELINGS WONDROUS KIND, CAN LOVE WITH FELINES EVER BIND, pen and ink, 9 ½ x 7 inches

Contents

Being Louis Benedict Cumberbatch	4
Introducing Louis Wain Chris Beetles	6
Catland: An Introduction to Louis Wain (1860-1939) Rodney Dale	42
Louis Wain's Fame: The Early Days	64
'Canine and Sublime': A Chat with Mr Louis Wain Roy Compton	65
How I Draw My Cats Written and Illustrated by Louis Wain	72
A Whole Pet World Louis Wain	82
How Animals Study their Appearance Louis Wain	90
'A Cat Society': The World of Louis Wain's Annuals, 1901-1921	96
The Musical Life of Louis Wain	100
Louis Wain on Law and Order	108
The Politics of Louis Wain	112
Louis Wain's Sporting Life	118
The Fashionable Louis Wain	126
Dining with Louis Wain	134
In Sickness and Health with Louis Wain	136
A Postcard from Louis Wain	140
The Late Work of Louis Wain	152
Louis Wain Lucky Futurist Mascots An Introduction David Wootton	208
Louis Wain Lucky Futurist Mascots A Catalogue Raisonné Compiled by David Wootton	213
The Life and Times of Louis Wain Compiled by Chris Beetles & David Wootton	230
Index	254

Being Louis
Benedict Cumberbatch

Chris Beetles' book is a joy, an inspiration and as thorough a document for understanding the life and times of Louis Wain as one could hope to read. So when asked to write the foreword to this new edition, having both played the man himself and produced the film *The Electrical Life of Louis Wain*, I jumped at the chance, only to realise that Chris, along with his generous inclusion of Rodney Dale and David Wootton's contributions, has covered so much that I was unsure what I could add. However, what I feel I can offer is perhaps the unique perspective of having tried to be this most singular of people and artists.

The experience of being Louis Wain and seeing the world through his eyes was a joy. I adored him and felt bereft when I had to leave him behind. He was such an acute observer, a skill that made him a master illustrator, but as Chris surmises brilliantly in these pages, there was a gap between this and the sense of him as an ineffective communicator. At these times it could be a deeply unsettling experience. To be Louis felt like tuning into a perpetual voice, sometimes quiet and shy, sometimes channelled into a singular focus, and at other times openly confrontational, a voice saying to the world, 'But don't you see?!'

His sheer energy consumption alone was something else. Only mellowed by severe depression, grief and eventually old age, his commitment was never-ending. His over-ambitious over-scheduling was certainly something I could relate to. However, his headspace was often far from chartered territory for me. His mind's wild and untethered nature could be freeing to play at times – a world outside the constraints of normality answerable only to him and his self-imposed standards. And then at other times rather terrifying – such as when failing as the responsible breadwinner for a large family of sisters, a situation which was all too frequent during his life. It's at these moments that I would feel the walls coming in as the real-world demands proved to be too heavy a burden for his slight grasp on reality.

Despite this frequent collision between Louis's perception of reality and the way things were, his achievements were astonishing. I think Louis was, in his own way, quietly revolutionary. Not least in that he married Emily Richardson for love. She was his sisters' governess, who was both outside his class and over a decade older. They both had to bear the brunt of the familial and social rejection that ensued. He also pursued several hobbies in his youth with the commitment and vigour and certainty of a prophet, whether it was boxing, improvising on the piano, dancing, chemistry, composing an opera or drawing inventions. Nobody could persuade him that he was going about things the difficult way or pursuing impossible targets with a limited ability. Not least perhaps because in one field he truly was a master: art, drawing and painting. He was also fast and prolific, and yet neither quality seemed to diminish the excellent results. Perhaps that is why he felt he could apply the same zeal to all of his activities. I certainly sensed that this was masking a great deal of self-doubt and uncertainty.

Louis's singularity, if you will, resulted in an authentic, unique, if at times perverse, point of view on all things. He was an artist who theorised, a boxer who improvised piano, a man seeking solitude who become fixated on his sisters' governess. A person for whom every high and every success seemed to precipitate a contingent low and connected disaster. Everything for Louis Wain sings with extremity. In moments of ill health or deterioration of circumstances or both, everything seems to blur in a kaleidoscopic mess of electricity, cats, love, loss of control and chaos. This arena of unhinged anxiety was a terrifying, rudderless place to occupy. And, ultimately, very lonely. What he carried through his life – along with his talents and capacity for love and compassion – were the confusion and terror of a little boy who knew he didn't fit in; a hare-lipped and sickly child who had recurring nightmares or, as he put it, 'visions of extraordinary complexity', which ceased after recovering from scarlet fever at the age of nine, but left him 'strong and pugnacious and difficult to control'. And this, if truth be told, I found profoundly sad and moving. Especially as the moment of finding a soulmate was then cruelly snatched away.

Somehow, despite the seemingly endless base note of loss and isolation, Louis's life was often uplifting and inspiring. He brought such beauty and celebration and joy to the lives of so many people. His gift was his eye and imagination, creating what the great H.G. Wells described as 'an entire cat world'.

Louis's lack of business acumen and worldly naivety, as examined in these pages and our film, meant that he failed to capitalise on his enormous popularity. By failing to copyright his images – which he mainly sold for a one-off fee – he became easy prey for the meaner opportunists in this new commercial age of mass reproduction. And equally tragic, if not more so in regards to his own sense of self-worth, was his inability to comprehend the importance of what he had achieved.

Considering this and how 'odd' Louis's art and life were at times, there is no doubt that in creating this world filled with his very particular brand of cat, Louis accomplished two extraordinary things.

Firstly, he actually changed how we view the cat. Because of his art and dedication to these animals, cats were elevated from being little more than pest control to being celebrated as the extraordinary, mysterious, amusing, fierce, affectionate, independent and truly complex feline friends they remain today.

Secondly, and most impressively (for me, at least), was how Louis, in trying to characterise a cat's nature in his anthropomorphic realisation of them in various social situations, leisure activities or political polemics, ended up reflecting his and our own human nature. He succeeded in fulfilling his own edict for the artist to observe and respond to his time and environment and 'be a very mirror held up to the nature amongst which he moves'. He brought them inside the home, closer than their distancing history of being worshipped as mystical gods or feared as evil allies of witchery and sin had allowed them previously. So close that they became acceptable as pets. And in observing their behaviour in the domestic environment, they are seen to be, as our film version of Emily Richardson puts it, 'ridiculous, silly and cuddly and lonely and frightened and brave – like us'. She goes on to say:

> Just remember that, however hard things get, however much you feel that you are struggling, the world is full of beauty, and it's up to you to capture it, Louis, to look and to share it with as many people as you can. You are a prism, through which that beam of life refracts.

It doesn't matter to me whether Emily ever said those beautiful words of encouragement from Will Sharpe's wonderful script that Claire Foy then delivers so perfectly. From that moment, I believed they were his life's ambition. Come what may, this is for me the sentiment at the beating heart of Louis's purpose. *To capture the beauty and share it with as many people as you can.* And somehow, amidst all the fog and terror of uncertainty and ill health, the growing confusion in an ever-louder world and in amongst all the grieving, the loss of mind and the years in the pauper ward of Springfield Mental Hospital in Tooting, I feel Emily stayed in his heart and mind throughout.

In the final years of Louis's life, an extraordinary group including H.G. Wells and the king raised money and campaigned for him to be raised out of obscurity and squalor, and gave him and his family some dignity. This lifted him up as he made his way to the finishing line. Reminding him and us that he achieved what Emily said was his life's purpose.

I hope that our film and Chris's superb work in these pages will move you, and in turn inspire all of us to view the Louis Wains of our world – the stranger, the oddball, the outsider, the round peg in a square hole – with more love and tenderness and compassion. Something we could all do with more of, for ourselves and each other, during life's journey and especially near its end.

Introducing Louis Wain
Chris Beetles

'Louis Wain invented a cat style, a cat society, a whole cat world'. These words written by H G Wells were broadcast in 1925. The great author of *The Time Machine* characteristically foretold the future of the Wain cat, which has become the century's most recognisable image in cat art. In 1925, however, H G Wells was describing a current and popular phenomenon: a cat artist who had become a household name over the previous 40 years and was reproduced in thousands of books, magazines, posters and postcards.

During their heyday, in the time before the First World War, Louis Wain's cats, dressed as humans, portrayed that stylish Edwardian world having fun; at restaurants and tea parties, going to the Races and the Seaside, celebrating at Christmas and Birthdays, and disporting themselves with exuberant games of tennis, bowls, cricket and football. It is this flamboyant portrayal of an age that appeals in turn to succeeding generations who recognise in it the energetic desire of a society at leisure. This is an exciting world of cats at play, uninhibited and slightly dangerous, with most group activities likely to turn into mishap, mayhem and catastrophe. This is Wain's world: funny, edgy and animated – a 'whole cat world'.

Louis Wain was born in 1860, a shy and eccentric personality who would become famous by the age of 40. At his most productive, he painted six hundred cat pictures a year, and published his celebrated Louis Wain's Annuals (1901 to 1921).

His working life spans the great age of the postcard and the prolific dissemination of his art in this way made him one of the most prevalent and recognisable artists of the early twentieth century. Between 1900 and 1940, 75 different publishers produced over 1100 of his images in postcard form.

His post-war financial difficulties may have contributed to a rapid decline into

Above left: THE LUCKY SPHINX CAT, LUCKY FUTURIST MASCOT CAT, 1914, ceramic, 5 inches high

Left: THE DAILY MEOWER
red crayon, 15 x 10 inches
This is an early period drawing in red crayon showing high quality draughtsmanship. Wain's first cat, Peter the Great, was taught the trick of wearing spectacles and peering at a postcard to amuse his wife, Emily.

schizophrenia as Wain became isolated, impecunious and unmanageable. In 1924, he was certified insane and admitted to Springfield Hospital. Briefly forgotten, he was discovered in this paupers' asylum a year later and, following a public appeal involving many writers and artists, and the intervention of the Prime Minister himself, he was transferred to the more congenial Bethlem Hospital and then, five years later, to the new Napsbury Hospital, in the Hertfordshire countryside. In these pleasant surroundings, he lived on until 1939, painting ceaselessly and recreating a new and ever more colourful cat world.

His later, unpublished work is now well known to us as it reveals his schizophrenic illness: highly coloured cats at times become frenzied and the pictures are often crammed with paranoid delusional writing: cats can show anger and are more intermittently frenetic, and often seen in the background are curious recreated

DERBY DAY – HERE THEY COME
pen and ink with crayon, 19 x 28 ½ inches
Wain's *Derby Day* is a nod to the large satirical social panorama exhibited by William Powell Frith at the Royal Academy, in 1858, to vast crowds and continuing popular fame. This is a typical set piece of cats behaving badly in public; uninhibited and cheerfully degenerate feline displays were eagerly taken up by Wain's fans in a spirit of self mockery since he had his first big picture published in the Christmas issue of *The Illustrated London News* in 1886 – *A Kittens' Christmas Party* – showing 150 cats celebrating the festival.

Left: CAT WITH CAT'S HEAD NECKLACE
watercolour and bodycolour, 7 x 5 inches
This is a classic example of Wain's late period of schizophrenic art. The ears, eyes and outline of a cat's head are incorporated into an overall symmetrical pattern perhaps inspired by the memory of his mother's Turkish-style textile designs.

Below: From a series of 21 Lucky Futurist Mascots, 1914-22, decorated with charms and Meow-Meow Notes.
From left to right: THE LUCKY KNIGHT ERRANT CAT, THE LUCKY BLACK CAT, THE LUCKY MASTER CAT [SMALL], THE DRINKING CAT and THE LUCKY PIG
1914, ceramic, various sizes

buildings, part-inspired by his mental asylums. However, there must have been periods of great contentment, as these late pictures often reveal a beautiful tranquility, with animals living in harmony in bright utopian landscapes.

The first comprehensive exhibition of Wain's work was held at the Victoria and Albert Museum in London in 1972, and since then Louis Wain has steadily become more fashionable, his artwork and ephemera being collected worldwide. It was at that time in the early 1970s that I bought my first picture and became enamoured of the art and fascinated by Louis Wain's story. My passionate pursuit and obsessive chronicling of this original material may also be a suitable case for enquiry but, from the thousands of pictures

Right: EARLY SPANISH
watercolour and bodycolour, 7 x 5 inches
This intense late period design shows a spiky, wildly delightful, colourful cat. The odd disjunction of Wain's title for this image is another recurring feature at this time in his life.

Below: TIME FOR MILK
watercolour and bodycolour, 6 ¾ x 9 inches
This is a typical picture from the late Napsbury Hospital period, 1930-39, though the mock-Tudor buildings first appeared in Wain's art in the postcards of 1904.

that have gone through my hands, first as a collector, then as a dealer, I have been able to distill the best and most compelling imagery.

This study will show three hundred plates of richness and variety, all of which are reproduced faithfully from the original artwork.

The intention of this new book is to share my particular areas of delight in his work, such as the 'late' period and the ceramics, and to surpass in a welter of lively line and colour, the size, scope and impact of all previous biographies, including *Louis Wain. The Man Who Drew Cats* by Rodney Dale, which I first published 30 years ago. I have done this by making the artwork the central interest around which all written material is gathered, giving weight and space always to the primacy of the image.

Louis Wain's eventful and frustrating life history is followed chronologically and placed within the context of the interesting cultural, sporting, and tumultuous political headlines of the late Victorian and Edwardian eras. In this simplified form they can be read in conjunction with Rodney Dale's comprehensive biography.

This volume further seeks to update all information as it has emerged over the years, and with that in mind I have invited Rodney Dale to update his extended essay 'Catland', published in book form by Duckworth in 1977, and which has since become a rarity. I am pleased that he re-presents these ideas with some interesting additions, adjustments and new images.

This is a profusely illustrated book that allows this singular artist to speak for himself through his art, but in simple terms his output can be recognised in three distinct phases: Early, Middle/Popular and Late Asylum pieces, and this volume loosely demarcates these areas.

CHRISTMAS CAROLS
oil on canvas, 22 x 46 ½ inches
This was produced as a print in 1889 to be presented with the December issue of *Myra's Threepenny Journal*. Since 1886 and the appearance of *A Kittens' Christmas Party*, anthropomorphic cats expressed human emotions of choral harmony. However, in this major work in oils, cats are still largely naturalistic and redolent of the Belgian cat artist, Henriette Ronner-Knip (1821-1909), of whose work Louis Wain was aware.

Facing page: ALL AT SEA
watercolour and bodycolour
8 x 7 inches
One of the five sisters that Wain had supported, Claire lived on to 1945 and recalled, 'Sometimes, London seemed to get upon his nerves and he would go off to Margate, there to spend an open-air week-end with the fishermen, running, swimming, boating and bathing with the enthusiasm of a youth'.

Above left and above right:
THE DRIVE
pen and ink with bodycolour
14 x 21 inches (with a same size chromolithograph)
This is one of a set of four large pen and ink designs, which were produced as an enormously successful series of chromolithographs (bright colours were added at the printing stage) during the pre First World War days of Edwardian England when golf (especially in Scotland!) became so popular amongst the leisured class.

Below: These are two large pen and ink pictures produced as prints in about 1910. It is a typical example of Wain's humour – cranky, ironic and never far from slapstick pandemonium.

Below left: A FREE LECTURE IN CATVILLE. THE LEARNED PROFESSOR WAS EXPOUNDING HIS THEORIES TO AN ATTENTIVE AUDIENCE (LECTURE OF THE NIGHT AIR ON THE VOICE)
pen and ink, 13 x 21 inches

Below right: WHEN SUDDENLY THE LECTURE PLATFORM CAME TOO HOT TO HOLD HIM
pen and ink, 13 x 21 inches

Above left: HOW'S THAT, UMPIRE?!
watercolour, 18 x 12 inches

Above right: A PERFECT FIT GUARANTEED FOR ONE AND ALL
MASHER: 'I CALL THAT PERFECTLY INSULTING!'
pen and ink, 14 ¼ x 11 inches
This is a typical example of Wain's social satire in which he gently pokes fun at the popularity of pre-war fashions encouraged by exaggerated advertising. This was illustrated in the 1915 *Louis Wain's Annual*.

Facing page: THE MEWSICAL FAMILY PLAY 'MEET US BY MOONLIGHT'
watercolour with bodycolour, 17 x 14 inches
At the age of 19, Wain studied counterpoint and harmony with a view to a musical career, and remained devoted to music throughout his life. Cats often appear playing musical instruments in his pictures, both solo and in bands. Alfred Praga (1867-1939), the miniaturist, remembers Wain in his Bohemian days at Phil May's 'Sunday Evenings' at his studio, where Wain loved to entertain and improvise at the piano.

Facing page: SPORTING CATS
watercolour and bodycolour, 9 ½ x 12 inches
Wain loved all sports: cricket, football, polo, croquet, bowls, golf and especially tennis and rowing in both of which he keenly participated. When he moved to Westgate-on-Sea in 1895 he named his house Bendigo Lodge after William 'Bendigo' Thompson (1811-1880), the infamous bare-knuckle fighter. He was himself a keen boxer and ringside patron and took lessons from Jem Mace, the ex-pugilist.

Above left: AND ALL THIS WETTING FOR ONE OLD BOOT!!!
pen ink and watercolour, 13 ½ x 10 ¼ inches
This was a best-selling postcard design.

Above right: OWZAT
pen ink and watercolour, 16 ½ x 12 ½ inches
This was a popular postcard from Wain's heyday, 1900-15, but represents a mania that may have presaged future distress.

Left: HANGING THE HOLLY
oil on board, 20 x 15 inches
This was part of the ward decorations at Napsbury Hospital, which Louis Wain painted every Christmas between 1930 and 1939.

Facing page: HOUSE DECORATIONS
watercolour, 9 x 12 inches
As he grew up, Wain was surrounded by colour. His father was a travelling salesman in textiles, his maternal grandfather a tapestry designer, and his mother a designer of patterns for Turkish-style carpets and ecclesiastical fabrics.

Facing page, clockwise from top left:
This is a group of four late works, typically pretty but densely coloured, with strongly structured compositions.

ON THE BALCONY
watercolour with bodycolour, 11 x 15 inches

WHO'S FOR TENNIS?!
watercolour and bodycolour, 7 ¼ x 9 ½ inches
Wain was a keen member of the Westgate-on-Sea Tennis Club and is remembered for turning up at its informal dances in white tie and tails.

CRICK'HIT OUTED!
watercolour, 9 x 7 inches
Late works sometimes show features of psychosis with strange titles such as this, jagged 'electrified' cats, and marginal scribblings of disordered thought: 'tight grip energies acts in a cats fur, spiking grim in pint to allow a wicket hit, when out goes the cat, broken from its clear course, chasn'd back aground on all fours, once in it soundly mounts, by beating the ball in runs'.

GOLFING CATS
watercolour and bodycolour, 9 x 7 inches
Though this is a later work in style, Wain would often return to the content of his early postcard designs.

Above left and above right:
These are two later works indicating a happy indulgence in activities and pastimes in the asylum.

PLAYING BILLIARDS
watercolour and bodycolour, 7 x 9 inches

TUG OF WAR
watercolour and bodycolour, 7 x 9 inches

Left: Henriette Ronner
BANJO
Louis Wain's earliest work, well into the 1890s, is competent, naturalistic and fits within the illustrative styles of the time. Wain acknowledged the work of Henriette Ronner (which is exemplified here), and in his more sweetly descriptive pieces her inspiration is present.

Below left: SIX CAT STUDIES
pen and ink, size unknown

Below: PRIZE CATS
pen and ink, 20 x 24 inches
In this 'early' period until the turn of the century there can be seen a lingering debt to many of the popular Victorian cat artists, in the treatment and subject matter, where cruelty, confrontation and chaos are never far away.

NOW THEN WHO'S MASTER?
oil on canvas, 30 ½ x 23 inches
Louis Wain involved himself in the late nineteenth-century movement to legislate against the routine muzzling of dogs. A variation of this image was used as a postcard in 'The Comical Cat Series' in 1904 with the title The Intruder.

By this time, Wain was shedding the object-filled interiors of genre pictures, and substituting natural animal mischief for a glimmer of human emotion.

Clockwise from top left:
THE PUNCH AND JUDY SHOW
grisaille, 18 ½ x 21 inches

THE GHOST STORY
grisaille, 11 x 16 ½ inches

ON THE BEACH
pen ink, watercolour and bodycolour, 16 ½ x 27 inches

DRIVING ME CRAZY
pen and ink, 12 x 20 inches

Facing page: TAKING SHELTER
OR 'POSSESSION IS NINE-TENTHS OF THE LAW'
grisaille, 14 ½ x 10 ½ inches
Published in *The Illustrated London News*, February 1887

Above: WATCHING THE MOUSETRAP
oil on board, 8 x 10 inches

Facing page: WATCHING THE BUTTERFLY
oil on board, 8 ½ x 11 inches

Above: **Harrison Weir**
EXIT STAGE LEFT
Anthropomorphic art had been enjoyed for centuries, so there was nothing new in Wain's first cat antics for a Victorian society familiar with such work as this by Harrison Weir (1824-1906).

Left: CAT IN A GLADSTONE BAG
oil on board, 8 ½ x 11 inches

ICE SLIDE
oil on card
23 x 18 inches
Oil painting came as easily to Wain as work in other media but he used it on fewer occasions as he became more successful later in his career. Speed of production against editorial and financial deadlines dictated this emphasis, but he sometimes gave time to a major work in oil as in the remarkable *Ice Slide* in which there is a memory of the panoramic conversation pieces of a previous age.

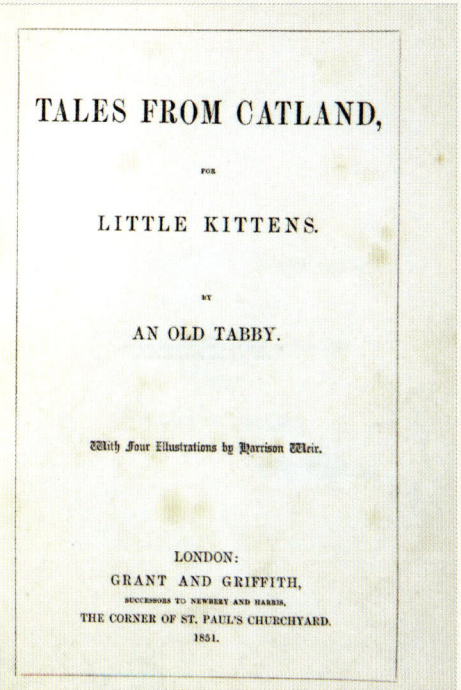

Harrison Weir
TALES FROM CATLAND

Above left: Looking at Weir's plates in *Tales from Catland* published in 1851, it can be seen that the images of cats in *Madame Tabby's Establishment*, a popular Wain book from 1886, are not particularly original and merely fit within the graphic style and cat iconography of the time.

Above right: At that time it was difficult for staff artists of the popular magazines such as *Punch* or *The Illustrated London News* (*ILN*) to have a distinct and recognisable appearance, for between their original artwork and the eventual published image were placed the wood-engravers (the *ILN* did not routinely use photomechanical reproduction until 1888). Even so, the distinctive humour in the Wain imagery was becoming widely recognised. An editorial comment in the *ILN* to accompany his sketches of the 'Cat Show at Crystal Palace' in October 1883, is revealing: 'our artist has exercised his wonted comic fancy, in delivering some incidents of this particular exhibition'. So there is an emerging element of Wain's comic reportage as early as this, and an evolution of his trademark look emerges and distinguishes itself from the prevailing vernacular of animal art. This was given further freedom from the standardising effect of the wood-engravers' interpretation as this profession became redundant in the face of the speed and verisimilitude of 'process' or photographic engraving.

In that era, when he was starting to become very popular, an artist craftsman no longer stood between Wain's pencil and watercolour drawing and what the eager public would then see on the page of their magazine. The art of Louis Wain was now fully released in all its characteristic racy energy and in full colour reproduction by the new and inventive print technology of the early Edwardian age.

From the mid-1890s there followed a significant phase of great fame and some transient fortune: the age of Wain as the cat artist without equal, all brought about by the mass production and distribution of his books, annuals and particularly his postcards, which penetrated every literate household in the land.

From then until the restrictive years of the First World War the cat cavalcade of typical Wain types would be seen everywhere from billboards advertising tea by Jackson's of Piccadilly to jigsaws in the toyshops.

Left: Louis Wain was the perfect one-stop artist for the ruthless entrepreneurial spirit of the age: a man who produced a seemingly endless output of cat pictures with novelty, yet was recognised within a well-established brand image; a predictably sound craftsman who would naively sell for a one-off fee and not retain his copyright. This was the perfect position for a merchandiser who would sell on the image for many different uses into a retail market that sought this Wain imagery imprinted on any object. With little risk then to the publisher in this brief fashionable period, a Wain mountain inevitably peaked in a crazy hot-potch of cat postcards, magazines, packaging, calendars and books, piled on top of toys, biscuit tins, and sets of domestic china. It had indeed become a whole fat cat world inhabited by wealthy purveyors of the secondary images of this artist, who was a man slipping inexorably from the saturated world of fame through familiarity into impecunious desperation.

While his health was sustained and his art was in vogue, his great artistic facility kept up with demand. His levels of skill allowed him to produce work in a great variety of media with fine control and unexpected impact.

Facing page: IT TAKES ALL SORTS
pen ink, watercolour, pencil and crayon, 9 ½ x 7 ½ inches
There seemed to be no medium that he had not mastered: from silverpoint pencil (pages 34-35) – a work of which Edward Burne-Jones would have been proud to have drawn – to large oils of cat gatherings in mock serious style, which were so suitable for the new pull-out supplements in magazines and for the volume print market demanded by an expanding literate consumer society.

TABBY FAMILY
silverpoint, 9 x 24 inches

Above: FOR WHAT WE ARE ABOUT TO RECEIVE
oil on canvas, size unknown

Below: FOR WHAT WE ARE ABOUT TO RECEIVE
chromolithograph, 6 ¼ x 19 inches
This print has the legend 'chromolithograph printed in Nuremberg from an original oil painting in possession of the publisher', and was illustrated in *Weldon's Illustrated Dressmaker*, Christmas 1894. This popular print is an early demonstration of Louis Wain selling off artwork and rights on an outright basis.

TABBY FAMILY
silverpoint, 9 x 24 inches

Above: FOR WHAT WE ARE ABOUT TO RECEIVE
oil on canvas, size unknown

Below: FOR WHAT WE ARE ABOUT TO RECEIVE
chromolithograph, 6 ¼ x 19 inches
This print has the legend 'chromolithograph printed in Nuremberg from an original oil painting in possession of the publisher', and was illustrated in *Weldon's Illustrated Dressmaker*, Christmas 1894. This popular print is an early demonstration of Louis Wain selling off artwork and rights on an outright basis.

Above: FIVE CHAMPION CATS
bodycolour, 15 x 22 inches
As an artist he was keen to please, and sought patrons especially amongst the titled and ennobled, and from dedicatory inscriptions it is plain that there was, either from anxiety or an irresistibly generous nature, no fee involved.

Right: FIVE KITTENS
watercolour and bodycolour
10 ¼ x 15 inches

Right: REVERSE OF FIVE KITTENS
(for obverse see page 37)

A mixture of skill, shyness and showmanship may explain the hundreds of examples of autograph book sketches, lively illustrated letters and pictures full of ambidextrous tricks and mirror writing that Wain left behind; a trail that leaves an impression of an impulsive and generous man.

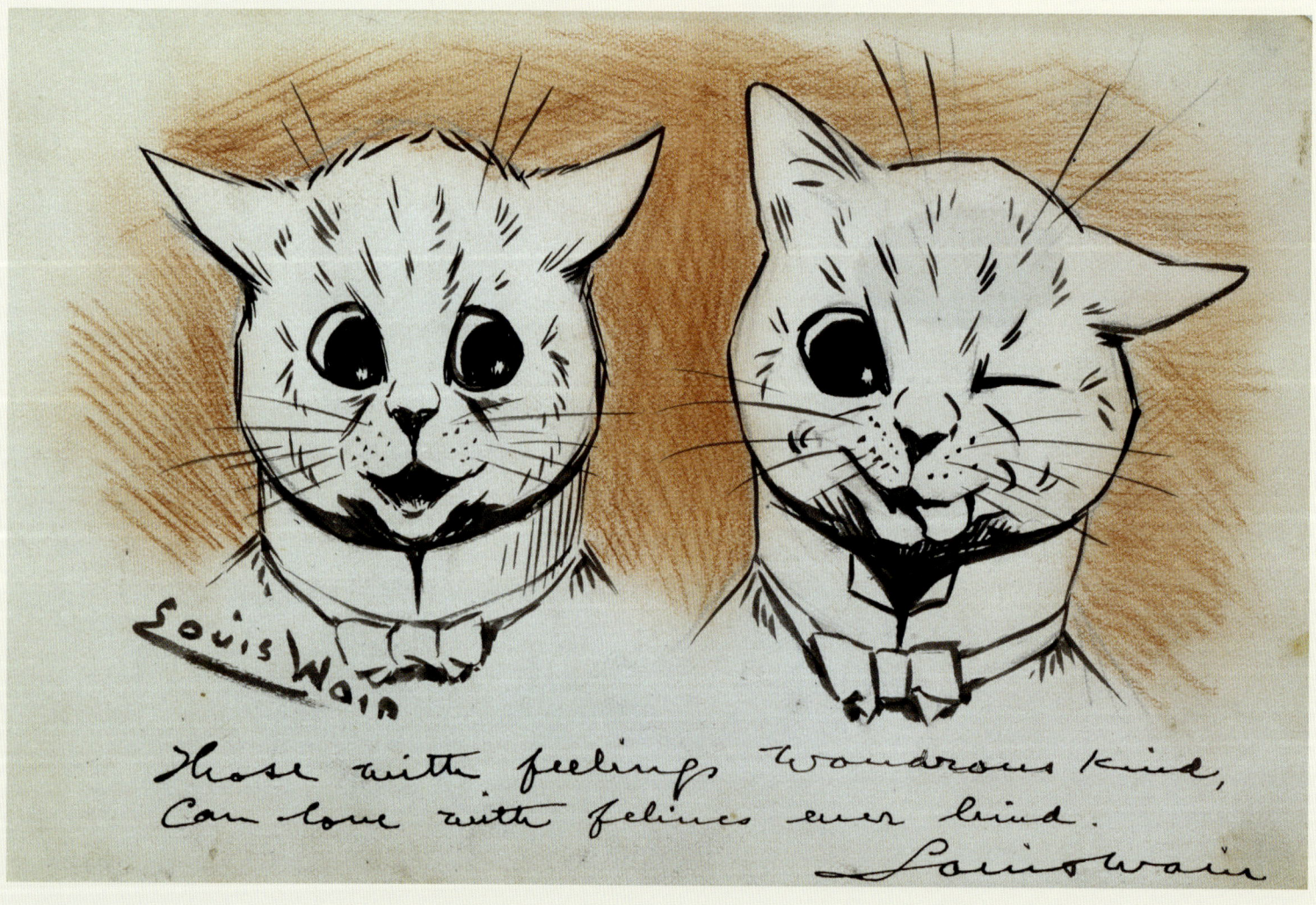

Facing page below: THOSE WITH FEELINGS
WONDROUS KIND,
CAN LOVE WITH FELINES EVER BIND
pen and ink, 9 ½ x 7 inches

Inset: CAT'S HEAD
pencil, 6 ½ x 6 ½ inches
From this rapid pencil sketch annotated by Wain it would seem that, to him, right-handedness was not the norm and was worth this demonstrative comment. Eye-witnesses are on record to say he could draw rapidly with both hands, sometimes simultaneously if requested. Rodney Dale in *The Man Who Drew Cats* (Chris Beetles Ltd, 2000, page 47) relates with fascination this torrent of unpaid cat impressions made on demand for charities, private parties, public gatherings, and passers by. He performed like a magician with a love of showmanship but so unlike a conjurer he gave everything away.

Above far left: THOSE WITH FEELINGS
WONDROUS KIND,
CAN LOVE WITH KITTENS EVER BIND
pen and ink, 8 ½ x 7 inches

Above left: GOOD GRACIOUS WHAT A SIGHT
pencil, 14 ½ x 9 inches
From the medical notes written when he was at Napsbury we know that 'he drew left handed, but signed his work with his right hand', and in the photograph on page 239 we can confirm this from his posture with his pen held in his left hand.

Above: BOTANIC GARDENS JUNE 28 1907
pencil, 8 x 6 ¼ inches

Without the restriction of secondary rights and the vigilance of a loyal and business-like agent, books and objects with Wain images proliferated; with the same pictures used many times over for child and adult markets, in multiple editions with different packaging and formats. The publishing industry, then as now, was a voracious machine obsessed with novelty, and Wain's pre-eminence was quickly eclipsed in the changing world of media delivery by overfamiliarity and evolving tastes. Amidst the thousands of books of varying quality there are still to be found unexpected pleasures. One such example is *Every Child's Own Picture Book* released in 1918 by Raphael Tuck in an inexpensive Father Tuck's 'Wonder' series with 24 adhesive stamps to complete the stories presented in verse form. With twelve pages, cardboard wrap-around covers and a fine four-colour plate picture of a dandified cat 'Setting the Fashion' as a frontispiece, it is a satisfying ensemble.

The fine artwork used (see facing page) incorporates two of Wain's strengths. One was his ability to create a lively story in three panels, perfected perhaps in the three years creating comic strips for Hearst Newspapers in the United States. Secondly there appears here good delineated examples of the animated episodes of what he called his 'dumpty' cats which were to subtly metamorphose into mascot cats in postcards (see page 145) and futuristic cubist cat ceramics the following year (see pages 213-229).

Louis Wain's struggle for consistent acknowledgement and financial success in his own lifetime are interestingly at odds with his acclaim a century later. Perhaps we live in a more empathetic society that is able to tolerate the eccentric and strange, the erratic and insistent artist whose personality obstructs a true assessment of his art. Indeed, in this age of superstar art, we may now be concentrating too much on the cult of artistic personality with journalistic blather ignoring works of true talent as it seeks ever more sensational excess.

The life of Louis Wain is one of frustration at the last with an existence always lived on the margin of a society unable to cope with his singular and damaged personality. It is easy to imagine the difficulties in doing business with him or befriending him in any sincere fashion. A steady professional life was denied to him by his own energetic flaws. Wain was the ultimate dilettante, ostentatiously interested in everything but truly knowing nothing, his theories and nostrums having no basis in scholarship or depth of study. Though always anxious to impress, he lived insecurely at the edge of true knowledge; he was 'everything by starts and nothing long'.

He inevitably became estranged from his family, rejected by editors, cheated by publishers and led the life of a loner able to establish only the briefest friendship based on self interest.

His public remained with him for a generation, but he was too unselfconscious to understand or maintain his popularity. However, he had by accident given the age the reassuring art it wanted and in turn it gave him a transient state of celebrity, until life, as it does, with change of health, fashion and world events, rolled over him.

Catland: An Introduction to Louis Wain (1860-1939)

Rodney Dale

'When I was young', said Louis Wain, 'no public man would have dared acknowledge himself a cat enthusiast; now even MPs can do so without danger of being laughed at.'

Raising the social status of the cat was due, in no small measure, to Louis Wain himself. It was more by accident than design that the inimitable Louis Wain cat was born but, having been born, its success was such that its procreator was hailed as an expert on cats, and found himself holding many influential positions in the Cat Fancy. He gave unstintingly of his time and support, and of what little money he had and, in spite of his unusual ideas of animal behaviour and care, 'Pussydom' prospered. He lived to be nearly 80 and, though he spent the last 15 years of his life in mental hospitals, it was therein that much of his most colourful and imaginative work was produced.

This essay surveys Louis Wain's life and art, helping us to evaluate how much the richer we are for it.

Louis Wain's father was one William Matthew Wain, whose career was in textiles. He was doing well in the family business when, to his father's dismay, he became attracted to Roman Catholicism. Disinherited, he turned his back on his native Leek, in Staffordshire, and moved to London, and it was through the Church that he met Julie Felicie Boiteux, an Anglo-French textile designer. Clearly, the two had much in common, and it was inevitable that they became husband and wife in 1859 and went to live in the Clerkenwell district of London.

The following year, their first child, Louis William, was born on 5 August. He was followed by five sisters: Caroline (1862–1915), Josephine (1864–1939), Marie (1867–1913), Claire (1868–1945), and Felicie (1871–1940).

It is clear that, from the start, Wain's view of the world was somewhat eccentric, with fuzzy boundaries between what was actually happening, what he thought was happening, and what he imagined might or could – or even ought to – be happening. In the following account, the quotations are from Wain himself, and you will see what I mean.

Wain was what was termed in Victorian times a 'sickly child'. He had a harelip (or cleft lip), a congenital condition nowadays rarely seen because it is corrected surgically with little difficulty. In his childhood, he suffered from terrifying recurring dreams – 'visions of extra-ordinary complexity'. However, at the age of nine, he contracted scarlet fever and from the time of his recovery he was never again haunted by visions. He wrote that, from then on, he grew 'strong and pugnacious and difficult to control'.

A CATS' PARTY
grisaille, 15 x 24 inches

His somewhat erratic schooling began at the Orchard Street Boys and Infant School in Well Street, South Hackney. According to his own account, he played truant often, visiting the docks, museums and Woolwich Arsenal, and embarking on nature rambles. From Orchard Street, he went to St Joseph's Academy, Kennington – a Roman Catholic Foundation.

He had some difficulty in deciding upon a career; his 'fancy trembled in the balance between music, painting, authorship and chemistry'. Finally, at the age of 17, he decided to become a musician, though evidence of his success is lacking. The compositions which he frequently said he had written – which included a full-length opera – are missing, and the only account we have of his musical ability is that he played wild, *agitato* piano improvisations.

Having studied both music and art, Wain decided that a career in art would provide an easier path to fame and fortune. But we have only his word for the way his career developed; later he wrote: 'I might in one sense say that I have had an art training all my life, for I never contemplated being anything but an artist in one form or another'.

For three years, he studied at the West London School of Art, and then stayed on as a member of staff. From what we know of his shy and retiring character this could hardly have been successful, and was certainly not in itself the path to fame and fortune. It was clear, however, that his sights were set on becoming a popular illustrator rather than a 'heavy' artist, and his stay at the WLSA

gave him an opportunity to build up a portfolio of work to show publishers and editors.

Two important events boosted his developing career. One was the death of his father in 1880, making Louis the family breadwinner. The other was his coming to the notice of Sir William Ingram, proprietor of the pioneering *The Illustrated London News* (*ILN*), which had been founded by Sir William's father, Herbert Ingram, in 1842. The magazine pioneered illustrated journalism; photography was not yet capable of providing what was needed, so Ingram employed teams of first-class artists and engravers to provide what was needed.

Wain's first published drawing (*Bullfinches on the Laurels*, erroneously entitled *Robin's Breakfast*) appeared in *The Illustrated Sporting and Dramatic News* (a sister paper to the *ILN*) on 10 December 1881. The following year Wain gave up teaching and joined the *ILN* staff to report on animal and agricultural shows. He would travel to a show, make notes, sketch the winners after the judging, travel home, and write and illustrate his report.

Facing page: THE NAUGHTY PUSS
chromolithograph, 18 x 27 ½ inches

He also visited places of interest, where another facet of his artistic skills would come to the fore. Since the pen is slower than the camera, the pressure on the illustrator-reporter of those days was very high. Many of Wain's drawings and reports are to be found in the pages of the *ILN* of those years (1882–86).

Although he needed solitude to work, Wain did not cut himself off from his family completely, particularly since the arrival of his sisters' governess, Emily Richardson. She was ten years older than he; nevertheless, they fell in love, went to live together, and then married in Hampstead on 30 January 1884 – Louis' twenty-fourth year.

Their happiness was short-lived. Emily was found to have cancer of the breast, and was soon confined to her bed. One of the diversions she had was a black and white kitten called Peter (1882-1898), and Louis would sit sketching him in all postures, hour after hour, to amuse Emily. She wanted him to show his cat drawings to the editors for whom he worked, but he feared that they would detract from his 'serious' illustration. When at last he did venture to show some, one comment was: 'Whoever would want to see a picture of a cat?' That was the end of that for the time being.

At this stage, he was still a very skilled general illustrator, but he had so many studies of Peter that the idea of 'working them up', as the phrase had it, was obviously an attractive one.

Sir William Ingram agreed. Wain had shown him some drawings including cats; Sir William published one or two of them and from then on kept a friendly eye on the young artist.

The break came in 1886. In that year, Wain drew some kitten illustrations for a children's book, *Madame Tabby's Establishment*. And that Christmas, Sir William commissioned a double-page narrative drawing for the *ILN*: *A Kittens' Christmas Party*. It took Wain 11 days to draw, and contains some two hundred cats (though some are very sketchy, but all are in the same vocabulary as those in *Madame Tabby*). It was an immediate success. According to Wain, it brought him 'overnight fame, and enquiries from all over the world' (which says something about the reach of the *ILN*). For the next quarter of a century, he was never short of a commission.

Sadly, Emily had little opportunity to share in her husband's sudden success, for, after long suffering, she died on 2 January 1887. But Louis Wain did not allow himself to become brooding and mournful. Emily's death was, after all, a 'merciful release', and his mind was diverted by the mounting demand for his work.

In the *Christmas Party* we see the beginnings of the Louis Wain cat, in the cat with a monocle making a speech, and the feline band which accompanies the dancing (particularly the harpist). As time went on, Wain's cats became more and more involved in human

Facing page: COMPOSER'S PARADE
pen ink, watercolour and bodycolour, size unknown

Below: THE MAYOR'S VISIT
watercolour and bodycolour, 7 x 8 ¾ inches

pursuits, while remaining firmly catlike. Then came the transition, in about 1890. The cats began to walk on their hind legs, don fancy neckwear, and sport monocles and walking sticks – the Louis Wain cat had been born. *A Cats' Party* (see page 43), published in the *ILN* in Christmas 1890 illustrates this very well.

As Louis Wain cats developed, they became more and more uncatlike in their behaviour, and more and more like naughty (or ingenious) children. But they were still undoubtedly cats. All Wain cats are somehow plausible, whatever they are doing. Certainly anyone who knows cats well will constantly see their Louis Wain-ness breaking through – it takes little imagination for a Wainophile (or a cat-lover) to see his cat sloping off – ostensibly for a round of golf or to take part in one of a range of sports.

So, from the 1890s, Louis Wain cats appear in action-packed panoramas, sometimes dozens of them in running battle with one another or with the dogs, the ghastly outcome of which can only be conjectured. His skill in conveying expression on the cats' faces is astonishing – in *Composer's Parade* – we see the whole range: surprise, concentration, determination, frustration, and more.

Very seldom are the cats represented as direct caricatures of humans. One exception in this book is *The Mayor's Visit*, which shows how devastating Louis Wain could be if he so wished.

One factor, not immediately apparent, which helps to make the Louis Wain cat credible, is its lack of clothes: when a Louis Wain cat wears clothes it is to underline some point in the picture. In *The Naughty Puss* (see page 44) for example, there is no doubt that the central figure, the one in charge, is the one with the frilly bonnet.

In *The Naughty Puss*, we see the stylised Dame School, with slates on which to write, the dunce with dunce's cap standing

Facing page: THE MOTOR ADVENTURE
pen ink, watercolour and bodycolour on tinted paper, size unknown

Below: THE LAND OF THE RISING SUN
watercolour with pen ink and bodycolour
13 ½ x 20 inches

in the corner, and a portrait of Our Founder (presumably), General Catty, looking sternly down at the scene. All the down-to-earth jokes are there – 'Miss Catty is a rat' written on the slate (hence the chastisement), and the map of Cattyland on the wall, divided into such provinces as Catsupshire, Mouseyshire, Tabbyshire and Manx Island. We must not forget to appreciate such pictures as historical records, and perhaps regret some of the changes that have taken place in our society in the last hundred or so years.

In the Japanese scene, *The Land of the Rising Sun*, the clothes emphasise the theme in a picture where everything is Japanese. In *All at Sea* (see page 12) the kittens wear bathing trunks to underline the seasideness of the scene – certainly not for modesty's sake, as will be understood from a glance at *The Motor Adventure*.

Louis Wain took little notice of the anatomy of the cat – probably it is as well that he did not, for he might then have found himself unable to draw some of the postures that he did. A critical and perceptive child once said, 'Mummy, they aren't cats, they haven't any bones'. That child was right; so many Louis Wain cats have india-rubber limbs and bodies, arranged as the picture demands with a breathtaking disregard for accuracy – yet somehow giving the beholder no qualms. *In the Vineyard* (see page 50) and *We Said We Were Playing Golf* (see page 51) are but two examples in this collection illustrating the bending of the cats' anatomy to the composition.

As we have seen, Louis Wain's object was not primarily to satirise either cats or humans: if there is satire in his pictures, it is usually incidental. His humour was straightforward, boisterous and Victorian. He wanted a vehicle for his playfulness, and for

one reason or another chose the cat, in much the same way as William Heath Robinson found absurd mechanical engineering a convenient peg on which to hang *his* playfulness.

There is a tendency to look for explanations where there may in fact be none, and some are adamant that Louis Wain was obsessed with cats because of Peter's association with Emily's terminal illness. I lend little credence to the story that he once confided to a friend that his late wife's soul had taken over Peter on her death. If that were the case (the belief, not the fact), he would perhaps have treated the cat with more reverence. And of course he did draw many other animals but, when you reflect on the topic, what other animal would be so suited to the many escapades Wain chose to illustrate?

Indeed, the Louis Wain cat conferred upon its 'onlie begetter' a fame of the sort today accorded to a 'personality' (usually with far less ability than Louis Wain). But, like a 'personality', his fame also gave him the false authority which goes with the breed. Because he drew cats, he must be an expert on them: accordingly, within five years of his *ILN* drawing, he found himself President of the National Cat Club, and many similar honours were to follow.

In that same year (1891), he was thought of so highly that he was mentioned in a book about the Dutch cat artist, Henriette Ronner (1821-1909), as being one of the few Englishmen 'who understand and appreciate feline beauty and feline character', though admittedly his cats were 'not of the character of [those of] Madame Ronner'. Ronner's compositions are suitable for chocolate-boxes, though her technique elevates her above that genre. Louis Wain admired her immensely, and copied at least one of her kitten drawings stroke by stroke.

However, honoured as he may have been, an expert on cats he definitely was not: he held distinctly strange ideas about them and their treatment. For example, he wrote of the cat:

> Here is an animal whose brain is in a transitory condition of development, whose sensorium in most specimens is not in a condition to withstand the shock of rapidly changing impressions without a severe mental strain which immediately reacts on the digestive organs. As a consequence, the cat will

cling to the original home, to the set of impressions the sensory nerve is most used to convey to the mind without effort, while it will suffer severe and obvious distress to the sensory organs when the sight is made to convey a number of strange and unusual scenes to them. The digestion suffers, the cat cannot eat well, and very often dies before the brain can recover its equilibrium.

The frailty of the cat's brain, however, has its uses. For example, when asked how it was that cats found their way home over incredible distances (and the truth of *that* belief is by no means irrefutable), Louis Wain replied that:

> The goal is so strongly impressed on the cat's brain that it is able to reason out its means and methods in order to reach it.

He continued:

> Strangely enough, I once had the impression that a cat's tendency was to travel north, and to face north as a magnet does, and that this tendency had some intimate association with the electrical strength of its fur.

Louis Wain was perhaps thinking of the 'electrical strength of the fur' when he drew *The Fire of Mind Agitates the Atmosphere* (see page 52) some 30 years later.

There are numerous other examples of his novel cat theories, but these will suffice for the present. It will not be surprising to find that Wain's ideas on other scientific topics were equally at variance with those commonly held. Although he said that he had 'studied the physical sciences', his drawings belie this.

He often said that he was working on 'several inventions' that he was patenting, but the records show three only, and they are 'provisional'. That being so, we shall never know their details, other than that he applied for patents on 'bicycles' and 'rangefinders'.

Facing page: IN THE VINEYARD
watercolour and bodycolour, 7 x 14 inches

Below left: COME BIRDIE COME
watercolour and bodycolour, 7 x 9 inches

Below right: WE SAID WE WERE PLAYING GOLF
watercolour and bodycolour, 9 1/4 x 12 inches

Wain's scientific studies are, in the main, just a part of his fantasy world. The life that he was living in the mid-1890s was sheer hard work. However, we have seen that Sir William Ingram had taken an interest in Louis Wain, and it was he, who owned property at Westgate-on-Sea (near Margate), who suggested that the Wain family might move to that town and be reunited.

Louis was a keen sportsman, specialising in boxing (he had been a pupil of the pugilist, Jem Mace, 1831-1910), and in fencing and athletics. He even went so far as to name the two houses in which they lived consecutively at Westgate 'Bendigo Lodge', after the prizefighter 'Bendigo' (William Thompson, 1811-1880) whom he much admired.

Having established himself as an artist, there was no need for Louis Wain to work quite so frantically, and he made the most of the opportunities offered by Westgate for swimming, fishing and boating. Sir William Ingram deserves our thanks for the help he undoubtedly gave the Wains.

THE FIRE OF MIND AGITATES THE ATMOSPHERE
ink and crayon, 13 ¼ x 10 ¼ inches

Although an artist, Louis Wain was always a journalist: his work was often topical, and crazes and events were reflected in the doings of his cats, as in his responses to innovation in aviation:

Aeroplane for Sale – at Any Old Price (see page 54) and *F is For Francis. He is gone for a flight/ in his big aeroplane to a very great height* (see page 55).

Come Birdie Come was a perennial theme of Wain's, based on C A White's very popular ballad of that title (1874):

Beautiful bird of spring has come
Seeking a place to build its home
Warbling a song so light and free
Beautiful bird, come live with me …
We will be happy, light and free
You shall be all the world to me
Come birdie come and live with me …

One is in little doubt of a mature cat's real intentions towards the beautiful bird. As far as the kittens in *The Canary Prima Donna* (see page 56) are concerned, they are clearly much less familiar with birds close up, and their expressions reflect their surprise and trepidation. The way that the lower left-hand cat is drawn craning forward is particularly skilful.

There is no doubt of the popularity of Louis Wain's work. In *The Book of the Cat* (1903), Frances Simpson wrote:

Facing page: IN THE VINEYARD
watercolour and bodycolour, 7 x 14 inches

Below left: COME BIRDIE COME
watercolour and bodycolour, 7 x 9 inches

Below right: WE SAID WE WERE PLAYING GOLF
watercolour and bodycolour, 9 1/4 x 12 inches

Wain's scientific studies are, in the main, just a part of his fantasy world. The life that he was living in the mid-1890s was sheer hard work. However, we have seen that Sir William Ingram had taken an interest in Louis Wain, and it was he, who owned property at Westgate-on-Sea (near Margate), who suggested that the Wain family might move to that town and be reunited.

Louis was a keen sportsman, specialising in boxing (he had been a pupil of the pugilist, Jem Mace, 1831-1910), and in fencing and athletics. He even went so far as to name the two houses in which they lived consecutively at Westgate 'Bendigo Lodge', after the prizefighter 'Bendigo' (William Thompson, 1811-1880) whom he much admired.

Having established himself as an artist, there was no need for Louis Wain to work quite so frantically, and he made the most of the opportunities offered by Westgate for swimming, fishing and boating. Sir William Ingram deserves our thanks for the help he undoubtedly gave the Wains.

THE FIRE OF MIND AGITATES THE ATMOSPHERE
ink and crayon, 13 ¼ x 10 ¼ inches

Although an artist, Louis Wain was always a journalist: his work was often topical, and crazes and events were reflected in the doings of his cats, as in his responses to innovation in aviation: *Aeroplane for Sale – at Any Old Price* (see page 54) and *F is For Francis. He is gone for a flight/ in his big aeroplane to a very great height* (see page 55).

Come Birdie Come was a perennial theme of Wain's, based on C A White's very popular ballad of that title (1874):

Beautiful bird of spring has come
Seeking a place to build its home
Warbling a song so light and free
Beautiful bird, come live with me …
We will be happy, light and free
You shall be all the world to me
Come birdie come and live with me …

One is in little doubt of a mature cat's real intentions towards the beautiful bird. As far as the kittens in *The Canary Prima Donna* (see page 56) are concerned, they are clearly much less familiar with birds close up, and their expressions reflect their surprise and trepidation. The way that the lower left-hand cat is drawn craning forward is particularly skilful.

There is no doubt of the popularity of Louis Wain's work. In *The Book of the Cat* (1903), Frances Simpson wrote:

PHRENOLOGY
pen and ink, 15 ¼ x 10 ¼ inches

In these latter days, who is there amongst us, young and old, who has not enjoyed a hearty laugh over the comical cats of Louis Wain? In his particular line, he is unique, for no one has ever portrayed cats in such various attitudes and with such deliciously expressive countenances. The adjectives and adverbs of the Cataract of Lodore would not suffice to describe the varied emotions of these funny felines. A Christmas without one of Louis Wain's clever catty pictures would be like a Christmas pudding without currants.

Between 1895 and 1905, some 40 books illustrated by Louis Wain appeared, many written by him as well. In the first few years of the twentieth century he produced several hundred postcards. Why did his fortunes decline when he would seem to be in his prime?

Louis Wain's downfall seems to have been his shyness, kindly nature and lack of business acumen. He sold his drawings outright, and was too diffident to negotiate the fees or royalties which he could have commanded. As a result, by 1907, although he was at the height of his fame, paradoxically he had the utmost difficulty in selling his work because there was so much of it already in circulation, freely used by editors as they wished. In that year, he was sued for debt, and judgment was entered against him. There was one way to try to redeem his fortune – to sail for a land where he would receive the welcome he deserved: America.

There, he worked for the Hearst Newspapers, drawing comic strips for three years. He seems, from his reports, to have been very impressed with America, and its Cat Fancy, and the American Cat Fancy was very impressed with Louis Wain.

In 1910, his mother died, and he returned to Westgate. Now, there were four sisters, for Marie (who died in 1913) had been in a local mental hospital since 1901. Caroline and Josephine kept house; Felicie and Claire, who had had some art training, discreetly pursued their work, though there was little fear of their eclipsing their brother's fame.

Fame, but not fortune. His return to this country found him as poor as when he had left: it is said that he invested all his savings in a wonderful oil lamp, which used hardly any fuel. The story goes that he returned from the United States resolved to patent and exploit the invention, but the war intervened. However, there is no record of his having attempted to patent anything and he had some four years in which to do it.

In 1914, he modelled some 'futurist' porcelain cats. According to one reviewer of their exhibition at Max Emanuel's showroom:

AEROPLANE FOR SALE – AT ANY OLD PRICE
pen and ink, 12 x 17 ½ inches

The futurist cat is the latest thing in freak ornaments. It has been evolved from the fertile brain of Mr Louis Wain, the inimitably cat expert, whose idea of applying the tenets of futurism to the construction of china cats has resulted in the creation of some truly wonderful feline fancies … It can truly be said at once that if not exactly things of beauty, they are a joy for ever. Yellow cats and blue cats, green cats and pink cats, and even pale heliotrope cats, were grouped on futurist shelves, and they were the quaintest, oddest tribe imaginable. Their faces, designed on crude cube lines, were the limit of grotesqueness, and were calculated to draw a laugh from the most miserable of men.

One set contained four cats, two dogs, two pigs and one 'grotesque'. He produced another set of somewhat larger models, one of which may currently be glimpsed fleetingly in the opening titles of *The Antiques Roadshow* (BBC1).

The First World War continued, and the Wains became poorer and poorer. Louis paid endless bills with his drawings, and many children and grandchildren of his creditors cherish his work today. There is no doubt that Louis Wain's private life was a great deal unhappier than his comical cats would seem to indicate. As noted

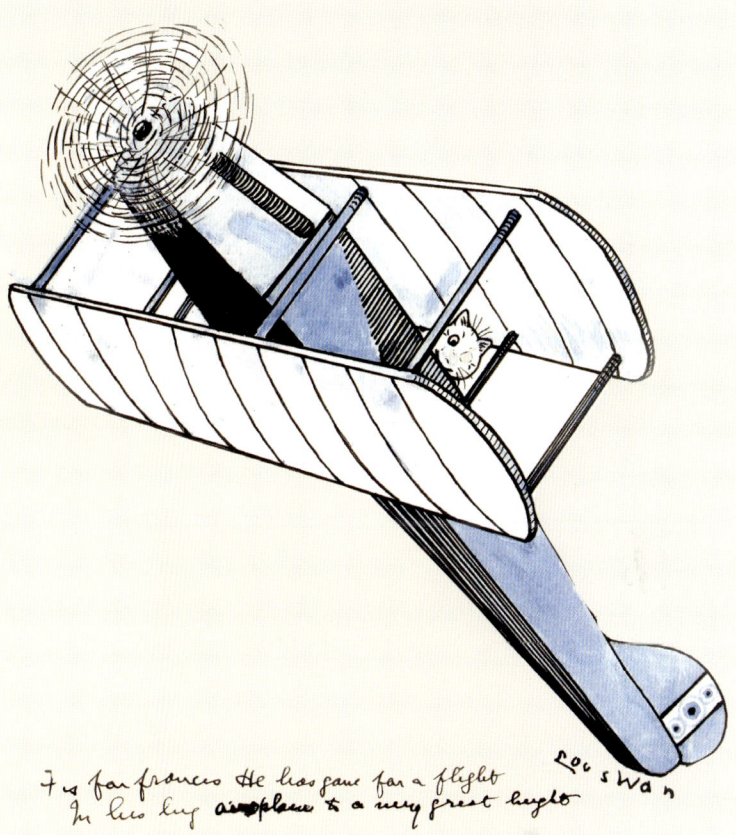

F IS FOR FRANCIS. HE IS GONE FOR A FLIGHT IN HIS BIG AEROPLANE TO A VERY GREAT HEIGHT
pen ink and watercolour with pencil, 10 x 8 inches

previously, his lack of business acumen, leading to chronic shortage of cash, had always been a constant source of worry – after all, he had four sisters to support. He was a famous man in his mid-fifties, yet a man whose work no one wanted except out of kindness. Any money he had made in America had gone on the lamp, or sunk – literally – with the china cats. The story goes that a boatload of these was torpedoed on its way to the United States.

In 1914, Wain lay unconscious in St Bartholemew's Hospital for a fortnight after falling from a bus in Bond Street. His fame was such that bulletins on his progress appeared in *The Times*. The legend was that the fall had been caused by a bus swerving to avoid – a cat. The war brought with it a shortage of paper so that fewer books were published. Louis Wain's career was apparently drawing to a close.

However, in 1916, he was approached by H D Wood, the British film producer, who asked him if he would draw an animated cartoon. Wain tried hard, but the venture was not a success; although he was a lightning sketcher, that facility is not necessarily what is needed for animated drawings.

In 1915, Wain's eldest sister Caroline died in the virulent influenza epidemic of that year. This loss affected him very deeply. The sounds of the War were a constant reminder of what was going on across the Channel. In 1917, the Wain family moved from Westgate back to London, to 41 Brondesbury Road, Kilburn.

Wain's reputation as an eccentric probably masked from his family and friends that his mind was failing. Friends became suspicious when he started canvassing their help for a non-existent cat show that he said he was organising, and talking excitedly of his scheme for breeding spotted cats. Then his delusions became more sinister – he believed that his surviving sisters had been responsible for Caroline's death, that they were stealing his cheques, robbing him, selling his possessions. Groups of spirits, he thought, were projecting currents so that he became full of electricity. He shut himself up in his room, writing frenziedly of his electrical and spiritualistic theories. He started to move the furniture about endlessly, believing that, by doing so, he would prevent its being taken away.

He became violent and liable to attack his sisters; they called for the doctor, and Louis Wain was certified insane on 16 June 1924. He was admitted to the pauper ward of Springfield Hospital, Tooting, where he was noted as being a man 'of a great many eccentricities, and possessed of many quite fantastic delusions'. However, he soon started to draw and paint: perhaps the rigours of the pauper asylum were a welcome change from the pressures of creditors and domestic responsibilities.

The diagnosis according to the understanding of the day was schizophrenia. We do not have space here to delve deeply into that condition, or the way that classifying mental illness has changed over the years; suffice it to say that all we know of Louis Wain's behaviour is consistent with the diagnosis. In 1966, Dr David Davies, Dean of the Institute of Psychiatry, wrote of Wain:

His childhood and adolescent fantasies; his fads, fancies and obsessions; his style of writing and his art; all are indicative of a schizoid personality, which finally ruled his life to such an extent that he had to be restrained.

With Louis removed from the family, his sisters sorted out his affairs as best they could, and started to capitalise on their own talents. Josephine ran the household. Claire and Felicie gave sketching-lessons, and produced some very attractive glass-paintings, fore-edge paintings (on books), and miniatures. Every week they visited Louis to take him materials and collect finished work for sale.

When Louis Wain had been at Springfield for just over a year, Dan Rider, a 'bookseller and publicist' who was also an asylum

Facing page: THE CANARY PRIMA DONNA
pen and ink, 5 x 8 ½ inches

visitor, earned his immortality by 'discovering' Louis Wain. This 'Dr Livingstone, I presume' story bears retelling. Rider wrote:

> I was on a committee that had to … visit … asylums. During one of those visits, I was passing up and down a corridor when I noticed a quiet little man drawing cats. I went to inspect his work.
> 'Good Lord, man, you draw like Louis Wain.'
> 'I *am* Louis Wain,' replied the patient.
> 'You're not, you know.' I exclaimed.
> 'But I am,' said the artist, and he was.

Plenty of people must have known that Louis Wain was there, but it was Rider's flair for publicity which enabled him to whip up the support needed and start a fund, so that within a week Louis had been transferred to a private room at Bethlem, with the attendant comforts of a rediscovered celebrity. Many people were surprised to find that he was still alive, since he had produced little published work in the previous decade.

Ramsay MacDonald, then Prime Minister, took a personal interest in the plight of the Wains – not only Louis, but his impoverished sisters. In his appeal for funds, he said:

> Louis Wain was on all our walls fifteen to twenty years ago. Probably no artist has given a greater number of young people pleasure than he has.

And in a later appeal, H G Wells wrote:

> He invented a cat style, a cat society, a whole cat world. English cats that do not look like Louis Wain cats are ashamed of themselves.

The *Daily Graphic* took a particular interest in the artist's plight, and started a fund for him and his sisters, but it was later found that an indeterminate sum had gone missing. Even so, sufficient funds were raised – and sufficient attention drawn to Wain's condition – for him to live in surroundings conducive to his starting to draw and paint again. (Further funds were forthcoming from exhibitions held in 1931 and 1937.)

The work that he was now producing in hospital differed from the hastily-produced cats for which he was, perhaps, chiefly remembered. He executed much work in watercolour and crayon, the colours became more exciting – sometimes to the point of crudity – and the ideas more daring.

Left: EARLY GREEK
watercolour and bodycolour, 7 ¼ x 5 inches

Facing page: ORANGE CAT AGAINST WALLPAPER
coloured pencil, 9 x 7 inches

In the past, there had been a series of familiar stock poses which we can see in this collection, but there are also some fine examples of Wain's new work. In the background of many of these later works we see strange architectural creations which he seemed to work into most of his outdoor scenes of the period.

Let us again turn to *We Said We Were Playing Golf* (see page 51). Perhaps the most interesting feature of the picture, which we have noted time and again, is the way that the cats retain their credibility while looking as no real cats can – all are anatomically unsound, and two are bright blue. The cat in the middle is sitting as one would presumably have to sit if one had a tail – the one on the right, however, would find the position more awkward. Two appear to have overcome the problem by sitting on boxes – in practice, this would be no help at all.

The opposable thumb, the feature which has allowed primates to rise above the rest of the animal kingdom, is here given to the cat world, allowing our subjects to hold things in an impossible, yet entirely credible, way. It is interesting that one of the items on the menu (where is the teapot, where are the cups?) is oranges. Louis Wain loved oranges, and friends and admirers sent them to him in hospital. But one of his theories had been:

> If you don't want puss to go near any given place, put orange-peel near this place. Cats will seldom scratch up any flower at the root of which the peel is put, and I have many a time known when they would not even cross a garden wall on top of which was a continuous line of peel.

In 1967, the late Tiggy McCrow and I conducted an experiment which seemed to refute this theory, and we came to the conclusion

YOU DARE!
watercolour with bodycolour and pencil, 11 ¼ x 9 inches

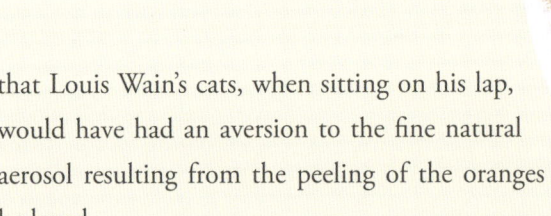

that Louis Wain's cats, when sitting on his lap, would have had an aversion to the fine natural aerosol resulting from the peeling of the oranges he loved.

From the same period as the golfing cats comes *The Fire of Mind Agitates the Atmosphere* (see page 52). This is an exceedingly powerful picture: red swirls emanate from the cats like the lines of force from magnets, made visible by means of iron filings. The cat on the left of the picture is clearly exercising an influence on the one on the right – and judging from the latter's expression, that influence is not beneficial. Perhaps this was a reflection of the artist's view of the world, that his body was charged with electricity, that ether – the source of all evil – was present in his food, and that he was filled with electricity and had magic powers of healing by the laying on of hands.

Another example from these later years are the so-called 'wallpaper cats', ranging from *Orange Cat Against Wallpaper* (see page 59) to *Early Greek* (see page 58), the latter being his own enigmatic title. Wain enjoyed experimenting with these patterns, but Fred Deuxberry, a charge nurse who became a great friend of Wain's at Napsbury, remembers his sisters coming to visit and complaining: 'we don't want that wallpaper rubbish'. There is some controversy surrounding wallpaper cats, of which he drew many. Simply, it has been asserted that the increasing complexity of the wallpaper, coupled with the deterioration of the cat, correlated with Louis Wain's mental state at the time he made the drawing. Apart from anything else, this would imply that the artwork provided a kind of 'mental thermometer' – but how would it be calibrated?

Certainly, we know that the filling of pictures with detailed designs is, in some cases, a manifestation of mental condition. There is no doubt that the artist's deterioration was more advanced when he drew *Sicilian* than it was when he drew *You Dare!*, for example. But what other factors might there have been?

Louis Wain's mother, we know, was a very talented designer of tapestries and fabrics. The initial design sketches for such works may be made on some sort of grid, and I have seen unfinished wallpaper studies of Wain's built up in 'fearful symmetry' on carefully drawn grids. It seems to me at least as reasonable to suppose that Louis Wain was experimenting with the patterns which he remembered from his youth, as that he was deteriorating.

One other possibility remains which I haven't mentioned before – Louis Wain was ambidextrous (though he usually drew

SICILIAN
watercolour and bodycolour, 7 ¼ x 5 inches

left-handed), and could mirror-write fluently. The art of drawing symmetrically using both hands is not difficult to acquire, and the pleasure to be gained from practising this technique may be the origin of some of these drawings.

One example from this period remains: *The Perfect Cat* (see page 62). Here, the rich decoration is most pronounced. Of this 'reddish-brown creature, mainly cat and part hare', Brian Reade writes:

> Around this conception of a *perfect cat* there spreads some dream-like foliage made the more vivid by the introduction of lilac shades amidst the green. In the background there is indicated the Alhambra in Spain. This place had a special significance because numerous cats were given a home there at the time, and Wain had published a drawing of it in the 1921 Annual, with the caption 'It is now the Cats' Palace'.

On the reverse of *The Perfect Cat* is an inscription in Wain's hand typical of his schizophrenic ramblings:

> The solitary one more real Persian cat is the one that is now going to be the one that is the real living animal left alone until the call is given to it at night time this evening at the same time as the rabbit can be again put to the test. This can be done by giving the call directly the light is seen after the first sleep is over … It is the perfect cat made the more perfect by the willingness given to it to be. The deer too can now be the same in the same way.

In May 1930, Louis Wain was moved from Bethlem to Napsbury Hospital, near St Albans. The buildings there were set

THE PERFECT CAT
bodycolour and chalk, 14 x 10 inches

in very spacious gardens and, although it took him some time to settle down, the doctors and nurses made life as pleasant as they could for him, and he received many visitors. He rewarded them with countless drawings, still treasured today.

It was not easy to communicate with Louis Wain at Napsbury, but his art was of as high a standard as it had ever been. At Christmas, he delighted in decorating the wards, with such images as *Cat with Blue Bow Tie*, and the custom arose of his decorating the ward mirrors.

His sisters continued to visit, bringing comforts, and taking work away. *Louis Wain's Great Big Midget Book* was published in 1935, but the material had appeared elsewhere, some of it dating back to the beginning of the century. The sisters were still able to support themselves in various ways with their art – for many years Claire demonstrated at exhibitions for the Royal Sovereign Pencil Co, drawing beautiful landscapes and seascapes to show off the different hardnesses of lead.

In November 1936, Louis Wain suffered a stroke which affected his speech and the right hand side of his body. In a few days, however, he was able to write with both hands, and drew a very good cat, using his left hand.

Josephine died at the beginning of 1939. Louis was not told, though he did ask why she had stopped sending him notes. However, the deception did not have to be carried on for long. By May, Louis was confined to his bed, incoherent and isolated. On 4 July 1939, he died of kidney failure and arteriosclerosis.

CAT WITH BLUE BOW TIE
watercolour and bodycolour on
board, 21 × 13 inches

His body was taken to the Church of the Sacred Heart, Quex Road, Kilburn; the following day Mass was said, and he was buried at St Mary's Roman Catholic Cemetery, Kensal Green, with his father and two of his sisters. Felicie joined them within a year, and Claire in 1945.

A memorial exhibition of Louis Wain's work was held in September 1939. The critic of *The Times* unwittingly wrote Wain's epitaph: 'As a man who gave simple pleasure to thousands, Mr Wain deserves to be remembered'.

But September 1939 was not a propitious time for memorial exhibitions – the world had other things on its mind and, when it had recovered, Louis Wain was forgotten. Forgotten, that is, as a public figure. Many private memories of him, and his works, were treasured by many thousands of people, lying dormant until the time was right for a revival.

I became interested in Louis Wain in 1966. In 1968, my *Louis Wain. The Man Who Drew Cats* was published; on the way I was surprised to find that I was writing the first full-length biography of the artist, and gratified, not only for myself but also for Louis Wain, at the interest it aroused. The Victoria and Albert Museum held an exhibition in the Christmas season 1972–73, the largest collection of Louis Wain's work ever assembled. Concurrent with this was the publication of V&A Keeper Brian Reade's excellent monograph on Louis Wain, putting the artist and his art into historical perspective.

Now, 80-plus years after Louis Wain's death, we have this new collection of his work. He who was a widely-adulated nine-days' wonder in his own time, and then forgotten for a generation or more, is now re-established with a solid reputation, properly based on some of his finest and most thoughtful work, rather than on the hasty sketches for which he was better known in his prime.

Louis Wain's Fame: The Early Days

The first serious account of this artist's life and artistic impact was achieved by Rodney Dale in *Louis Wain. The Man Who Drew Cats*, first published by William Kimber in 1968, without the benefit of colour plates. In this he found and referred to many primary sources. One of the most revealing and entertaining, though couched in the slightly melodramatic tones of the day, was an interview in 1896 written by Roy Compton for *The Idler* which we print here in full (see pages 65-70).

When Roy Compton set up this meeting with patient tenacity, the 35-year-old artist was already famous, and would, over the next 10 years, extend a vast penetration of the market for popular printed images through thousands of book and magazine illustrations and postcards. The interview appeared at the start of a period of energetic productivity, giving many insights into this pleasant working milieu where Louis Wain lived in almost dacha-like comfort, in Westgate-on-Sea, through the beneficial patronage of Sir William Ingram.

The article already reveals an established eccentricity of habit and demeanour that, in the pressured and conformist world of business, would isolate him from success in the years to come. A wide range of opinionated views are paraded, a style that was to intensify over the years in Louis Wain's prating articles in magazines and letters to the popular press. The characteristic gap between accurate observation (a talent that made him such a good illustrator) and interpretation (that made him such an ineffective communicator) is made plain. However, in one small ironic passage he is perspicacious, as a century later sound scientific studies show a strong correlation between healthy well-being and the tactile companionship of domestic pets.

"CANINE AND SUBLIME."
A CHAT WITH MR. LOUIS WAIN.
BY ROY COMPTON.

BENDIGO LODGE, WESTGATE.

I WISH to remark, by way of preface, that this is an upside-down interview. By rights it should have begun with Mr. Louis Wain and finished at his cats' tails; but when I reached aristocratic Westgate, a few days ago, and found myself in the cosy drawing-room of Bendigo Lodge, replying to the kindly welcome of Mr. Wain's mother and bright-eyed sisters, I learned that Mr. Wain himself was still in London, and the hour of his return was a matter of conjecture.

"I think, most probably, he will come down by the last train, go on to Margate, and run in from there."

"Run in," I remarked, surprisedly.

Mrs. Wain smiled. "Yes, he generally does so when he has had a laborious week; he finds the exercise does him good. So you must make yourself quite at home till he comes."

It would be difficult, indeed, to single out a more pleasant method of passing a couple of days than in Mr. Wain's cheery household at Bendigo Lodge. All the circle are so talented that, as Mrs. Wain naively remarks, "They have no time to be fashionable." She herself is the embodiment of kindness, with which is mingled a knowledge (practical) of the world, which has formed the nucleus of her son's success; it is to her he owes his artistic genius. Few churches or cathedrals in England but have some beautiful specimen of her work as a designer, for in that art she excels, and some of the finest Turkey carpets are woven from designs executed in the little triangular room through the windows of which you catch a splendid glimpse of blue sea.

Whilst Mrs. Wain has been chatting, she has drawn a basket-chair up to the

fire, and it is in the ruddy glow of the blazing logs that I am introduced to "Peter the Great," or "Good old Peter," as his master affectionately calls him. He is a black and white cat, once distinctly handsome, but the wear and tear of a public life have left their mark. He is of most amiable disposition and undoubted sagacity, and during his thirteen years of life has slowly, but surely, built up a name for the popular artist, who is willing to admit that it was the study of "Peter," and the portrayal of his antics, that first brought him public success and favour. Now the old cat dozes over the fire in peace—his every want attended to, his every wish gratified—a king amongst cats. I wonder as I gaze at him, with his eyes half-closed and his two fore-paws extended for warmth through the bars of the fender, if he realises that he has done more good than most human beings who are endowed not only with sense but brains; if in the firelight he sees the faces

of many a suffering little child whose hours of pain have been shortened by the recital of his tricks and the pictures of himself arranged in white cravat, dancing at a cat's tea-party, or gaily disporting himself upon a "see-saw." I feel inclined to wake him up and whisper how, one cold winter's night, I met a party of five little children, hatless and bootless, hurrying along from an East-end slum, and encouragingly saying to the youngest, who was crying from cold and hunger, "Come along, we'll get there soon." I followed them some distance down the lighted street, till they paused in front of a barber's shop, and I heard their voices change into a shout of merriment, for in the window was a crumpled Christmas

CATS' GHOSTS.

supplement, and Peter, in a frolicsome mood, was represented entertaining at a large cat's tea party. Hunger, cold, and misery were all dispelled. Who would not be a cat of Louis Wain's, capable of creating ten minutes' sunshine in a childish heart?

By the side of Peter sat "Bigit," a sleek, orange-coloured Siamese cat, with a strong penchant for poaching, which is gradually being eradicated under Peter's judicial eye.

A beautiful long-haired tabby, Leo, condescended to walk round me with stately grace, and it struck me how curiously dignified all the versatile artist's models were. They impressed you personally with the fact that they were not common cats. You might admire them, but any attempt at familiarity on your part would be instantly resented. Minna, another model, is a little French cat, a veritable La Parisienne, not only

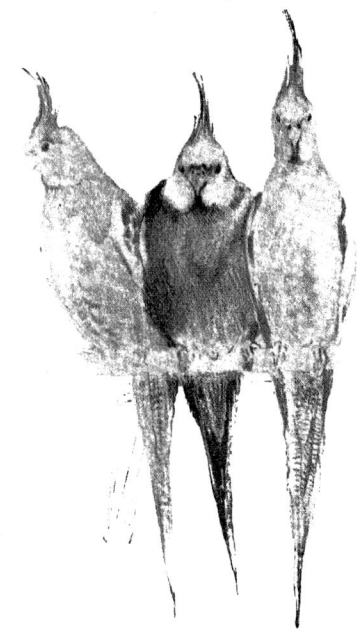

in appearance but in morals. And the circle closes with Rag-tag and Bob-tail, two dogs who have already won favourable criticism from the public.

The lunch-bell is ringing on the following day when Mr. Louis Wain himself appears. Agile and erect in figure, he is too true an artist to have professional affectations or conceits, and his manner is singularly unassuming and simple. It is over the walnuts I ask him to tell me a little about his career.

"I seriously started my artistic life at nineteen, after some years' training at the West London schools. Before that time I worked spasmodically at music, authorship, and chemistry. Finally art prevailed. My mother tells me that from my childhood I had always a great appreciation for colouring, and used to amuse myself for hours grouping shaded leaves.

My school life was dilatory; sometimes I would play truant for three months at a time, and my father would be unaware of the fact, till he received a long letter from the schoolmaster on the duty of parents, at which he would be greatly surprised, until half-way through the letter he learnt:—

'Your son has not been near school for three months!'"

"And your object in staying away?"

"A curious one. I was intensely fond of reading American Indian stories. The sagacity of the race, and their wonderful sight and keenness in following trails, all appealed strongly to my imagination. I used to wander in the parks study-

ing nature, and visited all the docks and museums. I consider that my boyish

fancy did much towards my future artistic life, for it taught me to use my powers of observation, and to concentrate my mind on the details of nature which I should otherwise never have noticed."

"But at first cats were not your forte?"

"No; but I have always been intensely fond of dumb animals. At first, like most men, I found it uphill work, and I had difficulty in obtaining a footing. I started by making sketches for *The Sporting and Dramatic News* at agricultural shows all over the country, and got a keen insight into rural life. It was Peter who first suggested to my mind my fanciful cat creations. I sat watching his antics one evening, and I did a small study of kittens, which was accepted by the *Lady's Pictorial*. Then I trained Peter like a child, and he became my principal model, and the pioneer of my success. He has helped to wipe out, once and for all, the contempt in which the cat has been held in this country, and raised its status from the questionable care and affection of the old maid to a real and permanent place in the home. I have myself found, as the result of many years of inquiry and study, that all people who keep cats, and are in the habit of nursing them, do not suffer from those petty little ailments which all flesh is heir to, viz., nervous complaints of a minor sort. Hysteria and rheumatism, too, are unknown, and all lovers of 'pussy' are of the sweetest temperament. When a student at home, I have often myself felt the benefit, after a long spell of mental effort, of my cats sitting across my shoulders, or of half-an-hour's chat with my pet, 'Peter.' Our English cats are slowly but surely developing into stronger types, which have very little affinity with the uncertain and unstable creature of the tiles and chimney-pots. With careful breeding the lank body and the long nose disappear, the face becomes condensed, as it were, into a series of circles, the expression develops artlessness, and the general temperament of the animal

"PETER."

MR. LOUIS WAIN.

is one of loving conceit. A marvellous change has also come about in the quality of both long and short-haired varieties, since the National Cat Club has taken such a strong hold on the public fancy."

"And your first big success, I remember, was the double-page of 'Cats' in the *Illustrated London News*?"

"Yes. I suggested the idea to Sir William Ingram, to whose kindly interest I owe the foundation of my success. He, in the first instance, had encouraged me greatly by taking some of my sketches which showed promise but were not sufficiently good to reproduce. I worked upon the 'Cats' picture eleven days, and it contained one hundred and fifty cats with varying expressions."

"And then the tide turned?"

"Yes. It caught the public fancy, and I have since had orders from all parts of the world."

"And your average work?"

"Is fourteen hours a day, but the moment I feel I am not doing justice to my subject, I lay aside my brush, and write a humorous story, or study chemistry."

"And how do you manage to accumulate so many humorous ideas?"

"I am always taking notes when engaged upon one sketch. I am also planning my next subject. Cats are not my only speciality; birds afford really a greater scope for expression and variety of ideas. Here is an owl," Mr. Wain remarks, handing me a sketch. "He was one of my models, and a most jealous individual. There was a stuffed owl in the room he lived in for which he entertained a desperate hatred, and one day he attacked and scratched it to pieces. The result was that he died suddenly from arsenical poisoning. I will fetch you some of my note-books and you can judge for yourself of the variety of black-and-white work that I undertake."

Mr. Wain reappears with an armful of note-books, and a block and a pencil on which he promises to make me a special sketch of a cat for the benefit of "THE IDLER." It is marvellous to note with what rapidity and ease he works.

"And do you think there is any future for the black-and-white man?" I ask, as I watch him work.

"Yes, a brilliant one. At the present moment he is his own enemy, for his tendency is to work in a groove instead of entering into the spirit of the age, and being sensitive to all its crazes, advancements, prejudices, and teachings. Personally, I work for every paper in turn, for I find from experience that if you work for one editor you get one class of ideas, and if you constantly change, you avoid degeneracy. A man should never allow his fancy to run away with his judgment. His sketches should be the result of accurate insight into and appreciation of the variety of characters he has to please; he should be a very mirror held up to the nature amongst which he moves.

"The prices given for black-and-white to-day compare very favourably with that of the last ten years, for then a drawing had to be accurately finished in every detail before being accepted."

Whilst Mr. Wain is talking, the cats' ghosts have appeared, and I leave in their good company.

MR. LOUIS WAIN.

"PETER."

MR. LOUIS WAIN.

is one of loving conceit. A marvellous change has also come about in the quality of both long and short-haired varieties, since the National Cat Club has taken such a strong hold on the public fancy."

"And your first big success, I remember, was the double-page of 'Cats' in the *Illustrated London News*?"

"Yes. I suggested the idea to Sir William Ingram, to whose kindly interest I owe the foundation of my success. He, in the first instance, had encouraged me greatly by taking some of my sketches which showed promise but were not sufficiently good to reproduce. I worked upon the 'Cats' picture eleven days, and it contained one hundred and fifty cats with varying expressions."

"And then the tide turned?"

"Yes. It caught the public fancy, and I have since had orders from all parts of the world."

"And your average work?"

"Is fourteen hours a day, but the moment I feel I am not doing justice to my subject, I lay aside my brush, and write a humorous story, or study chemistry."

"And how do you manage to accumulate so many humorous ideas?"

"I am always taking notes when engaged upon one sketch. I am also planning my next subject. Cats are not my only speciality; birds afford really a greater scope for expression and variety of ideas. Here is an owl," Mr. Wain remarks, handing me a sketch. "He was one of my models, and a most jealous individual. There was a stuffed owl in the room he lived in for which he entertained a desperate hatred, and one day he attacked and scratched it to pieces. The result was that he died suddenly from arsenical poisoning. I will fetch you some of my note-books and you can judge for yourself of the variety of black-and-white work that I undertake."

Mr. Wain reappears with an armful of note-books, and a block and a pencil on which he promises to make me a special sketch of a cat for the benefit of "THE IDLER." It is marvellous to note with what rapidity and ease he works.

"And do you think there is any future for the black-and-white man?" I ask, as I watch him work.

"Yes, a brilliant one. At the present moment he is his own enemy, for his tendency is to work in a groove instead of entering into the spirit of the age, and being sensitive to all its crazes, advancements, prejudices, and teachings. Personally, I work for every paper in turn, for I find from experience that if you work for one editor you get one class of ideas, and if you constantly change, you avoid degeneracy. A man should never allow his fancy to run away with his judgment. His sketches should be the result of accurate insight into and appreciation of the variety of characters he has to please; he should be a very mirror held up to the nature amongst which he moves.

"The prices given for black-and-white to-day compare very favourably with that of the last ten years, for then a drawing had to be accurately finished in every detail before being accepted."

Whilst Mr. Wain is talking, the cats' ghosts have appeared, and I leave in their good company.

MR. LOUIS WAIN.

Louis Wain, with three of his sisters and a friend, in the back garden of 7 Collingwood Terrace, Westgate-on-Sea

Published in *The School Girl's Annual*, 1922

HOW I DRAW MY CATS

Written and Illustrated by Louis Wain

It is difficult exactly to answer the question how I draw my cats, because it depends so much upon circumstances. For instance, I like to sit down for an hour's nature work at my own or other people's cats, and take the cats in whatever mood I find myself. Sometimes I sit down at my drawing-table without thinking at all of nature, and yet nature comes very frankly, if one is in the humour, without the model, that is, if one is drawing natural cats.

But the work that is done direct from nature is more vivid, more convincing, and takes only half the time. The drawing is freer, the light and shade more daring and natural, and there is nothing to compare with it for conveying nature.

There are, however, many, many moods to draw upon, and if I want to get a real laughing cat I cannot get it by going to nature direct. I must go to nature the *day before* and then keep the impression in my mind, and the mind models it into humorous guise with the strength of nature at the back of it.

But again, if I want a mild, irresponsible caricature, a grinning cat, then I have to let loose my nature impressions and let myself go on my own account, and it is astonishing what variety one can get in this way, and how one's moods vary from day to day. I have done as many as one hundred and fifty laughing cats at a time, no two being alike.

There is another way of sketching cats, and this way I often resort to. I take a sketchbook to a restaurant,

NO 2. THE SAME SKETCH WORKED UP WITH SHADOW AFTERWARDS. TIME TAKEN OVER DRAWING, TWO MINUTES AND A HALF

NO 1. A SKETCH FROM NATURE, SHOWING HOW THE ATTITUDE IS BLOCKED IN RAPIDLY IN A FEW STROKES. TIME TAKEN OVER DRAWING, ONE MINUTE

NO 3. THE SAME SKETCH WORKED IN BLACK AND WHITE. TIME TAKEN OVER DRAWING, FIVE MINUTES. TIME TAKEN OVER THREE DRAWINGS ALTOGETHER, EIGHT MINUTES AND A HALF. THE ORIGINALS WERE EXACTLY DOUBLE THE SIZE OF THESE REPRODUCTIONS

THREE LITTLE KITTENS

or other public place, and draw the people in their different positions *as cats*, getting as near to their human characteristics as possible. This gives me *doubly* nature, and these studies I think my best humorous work.

I am told that I am very serious over it, but as a matter of fact I am bubbling over with interior laughter until I am tired, not of drawing, but of laughing. It is a species of laughter which is very keen and absorbing, and carries one away from one's surroundings, and I often feel afterwards as if I am aching all over.

Sometimes I get this mood upon me when I am drawing at charity bazaars, when pace comes into my pencil, and I draw an extraordinary number of sketches in a very short time. But they are keen mind-impressions drawn at concert pitch and full of life, and I sometimes think that

AUTOGRAPH CAT

ONE EYE ON YOU

LAUGHING CAT

FACING PAGE: TWENTY CATS

CATS ARE BAD SITTERS IN THE ORDINARY SENSE

I should like to keep those sketches myself, as I cannot draw them under studio or other conditions as I can at these bazaars, and I have nothing by me to represent these moods. It is, as I might express it, the quintessence of expressed life, as far as one can go and remain reasonable.

I have, of course, gone through the usual artistic method of only working when the mood is upon me, but that was long ago.

One learns that the mood for work could be, can be, and always is able to be forced at all times, and a favourite method with me when I get tired in my work is to force the tiredness until the tiredness wears out and leaves me strong. This may sound paradoxical, but it is nevertheless the fact that tiredness does not always mean mental inability, or physical disability, but simply a slacking of all the energies through a lack of interested mental concentration. I would impress this seriously upon the reader, because normally good health, good spirits, and good work

AM I NOT HAPPY? I PASS SOME OF IT ON TO YOU

all depend upon a good mental concentration; in fact, it is the energising factor of all human effort, and if one falls away from it seriously, then everything goes wrong, work comes in moods, health wavers to unfitness, and the mind stagnates, and any aid to bring about mental concentration and interest is of supreme importance to the individual.

Sometimes the mind satiates with pencil or pen-and-ink work, and takes readily to colour as a relaxation, sometimes it is the other way about.

I have just done a whole series of strikingly novel cats to be produced as china cats. The marking of these cats was of the most extraordinary interest, and I could not leave them, day or night, until finished. First, because I had struck a novelty; secondly, because they gave me scope for striking expression; thirdly, because I never knew from one moment to another exactly what I was going to do. It was the expression of a mood and it all came out as a surprise to me.

One thing, however, is extraordinary; in drawing my cats, I always commence by drawing the ears first; in every case I do this, and if I try any other way the proportions are certain to go wrong. Why, I do not know. Whether it is mere habit, and I have grown into it as a habit difficult to break, or not, it remains the same; any unsatisfactory work comes when the ears have not been the first keynote of the drawing.

Again, I am in the habit of drawing at a table on a flat drawing-board, and if I take to an easel my work becomes quite different, almost as though it were done by another man. The easel begets greater strength of handling, freer work and better tonality, but not such careful drawing.

Then there is that wonderful 6B pencil drawing. There is nothing to compare with

THE MORE YOU WANT THEM QUIET THE MORE THEY MOVE

A ROUGH PENCIL SKETCH WITH A 6B PENCIL

without correction, one cannot rub out as one can pencil, and a wrong line spoils the whole drawing, and one cannot make a pencil study first of all to work over, as the pencil surface is slippery and will not take the chalk readily, and rubbing out with rubber spoils the paper for chalk. Consequently, when at rare intervals I work up to doing a red chalk drawing, I am loath to part with it, because it means so much.

the comfort of drawing and the freedom and strength of handling it gives; but, of course, you must thoroughly know your work, and have a firm grip of your pencil when doing it.

But perhaps the most taxing of all work is marking in red Venetian chalk, a sort of brown red, rich and strikingly beautiful. It pulls on the paper and makes one very tired working in it in consequence.

As my work is done at great pace, and every stroke has to be put in very accurately

ALL MY EYE!

Cats are bad sitters in the ordinary sense; the more you want to keep them quiet the more they will move, and the more you try the more suspicious you make them. They have their soft evening moods, however, and this is the best time for light and shade, and the best time to catch them. An occasional cat is vain enough to like being drawn, but the majority despise art and all its artful wiles.

A MOMENTARY IMPRESSION CAUGHT AND DASHED IN AT LIGHTNING SPEED

A KITTEN LINE

I'M LOOKING AT YOU

I WONDER

be fatal. You must rush while the impression of form is strong in your mind. Sometimes a sketch done in a few strokes will amplify afterwards at leisure in detail, and turn out well; but sometimes a more elaborate sketch spoils by an afterthought.

The surest way for the student to start drawing cats is to buy a shilling china cat model. It cannot run away!

I must have loved cats very much to have persuaded them to do all they have done for me. In drawing them you never know where you are, or where your work begins and ends. They are so fitful in their movements, you have to rush your pencil at its quickest pace and make strong, vivid, mental impressions. You cannot stop still to study – that would

WHICH DO I LOVE BEST?

THE ARTISTS

THE DEBUTANTE. HER FIRST SEASON

A Whole Pet World

P̲ublished in 1922 in *The School Girl's Annual*, 'How Animals Study Their Appearance' inadvertently reveals the common ground between Louis Wain, the arch-proponent of twentieth-century anthropomorphic art, and his millions of followers. He was, of course, a pet owner. 'Peter the Great', as he called him, was his first pet and he was the first of probably hundreds, all to become the unsung heroes of the domestic studio and the sketchbook.

Above: PETER

Left: STUDIES OF A SLEEPING TABBY

BEST OF CHUMS

In *The Idler* of 1896 (see pages 65-70) we were introduced to his first houseful of pets and many reports followed over the years of a well-stocked menagerie of dogs, cats and birds. He declared sincerely, 'I love all dumb animals' and, in turn, he invested them with human emotions and sought affection and human patterns of behaviour in response. It is a short step from sentimentality to the pleasure of anthropomorphism: a closely aligned way of thinking where incongruity causes reassuring mirth rather than revulsion or dismissal of the absurd.

As with many pet owners, Wain seemed to regard animals as an extended family, and liked to portray them acting in harmony. In the wild, of course, this harmony can be subverted by harsh

SIAMESE TWINS

natural law, which Wain recognised and dealt with in many a jokey animal skirmish. His world view was optimistic, and he believed that human beings should organise themselves for the common good. When he wasn't fruitlessly writing to the papers, he was more effectively able to express this view by displaying a coherent animal kingdom, a place of fantasy, where they could show good manners and finer feelings of concern for each other in an ideal world, where even the lion lies down with the lamb.

However, many of Wain's jokes and cartoons reflect the setbacks and disasters of his personal life. By nature naïve and trusting, he was prepared to see the good in everything, though his illustrative work is generally pessimistic in outcome. In his art he scatters incidents of disorganisation and instability which inevitably result in disaster. But this is the world of knockabout humour where participants are maimed just a little bit and no one dies, and it was all the more popular for that. In the threat inevitably lurking in a calamitous world, it is comforting to find control and methods of coping in the intrinsic humour of slapstick.

THE BODYGUARD

Facing page: THE INTRUDER

Above: WONT YOU GIVE ME A LITTLE OF YOUR MILK, PUSSY?

Right: I CANNOT EAT YOU DUCKLING DEAR

Above: THE NIGHT ATTACK
This design was first published by J Beagles & Co, circa 1904, in 'The Seven Ages' series of postcards, based on Jacques' famous speech in Shakespeare's *As You Like It*. Originally called *Then, a Soldier*, it was later re-issued as a postcard with this more populist title.

Facing page: UNLOADING THE PICNIC

Facing page: THE INTRUDER

Above: WONT YOU GIVE ME A LITTLE OF YOUR MILK, PUSSY?

Right: I CANNOT EAT YOU DUCKLING DEAR

Above: THE NIGHT ATTACK
This design was first published by J Beagles & Co, circa 1904, in 'The Seven Ages' series of postcards, based on Jacques' famous speech in Shakespeare's *As You Like It*. Originally called *Then, a Soldier*, it was later re-issued as a postcard with this more populist title.

Facing page: UNLOADING THE PICNIC

HOW ANIMALS STUDY THEIR APPEARANCE

By Louis Wain

Do people quite realise how proud cats are of their whiskers and how careful they are to keep them quite clean? Watch a cat drinking, and you will notice that it draws its whiskers quite back as a rule, in order that they shall not get wetted and soiled; note how the paws are afterwards stroked over the whiskers to brighten them up, and how the cat yawns to stretch the whiskers out again to air and dry them with one vigorous effort.

Some cats will starve themselves rather than eat soft food out of a big basin which is likely to soil the whiskers. The vanity of keeping their whiskers clean will often thus cause an illness through want of proper food, while the family is wondering what is the matter with poor

NOTICE THAT A CAT DRAWS ITS WHISKERS BACK AS A RULE WHEN DRINKING, IN ORDER THAT THEY SHALL NOT BE WETTED OR DIRTIED.

puss. See how a cat resents its whiskers being touched, and how soft it will become if it can make a great display of them from the eminence of the table.

To my mind the average cat thinks more of its whiskers than it does of its mistress or its home, and in many cases I am certain that it is a pet vanity. The cat's whiskers are tender and highly sensitive and sometimes vibrate with delight; they tell you what the cat is thinking about if you watch them carefully, for while the eyes are mystic, the whiskers give their owner away, and it is mostly vanity.

Vanity keeps the cat by one's side, vanity makes it rub and stroke against one's legs, a confident vanity which you cannot resist; love comes afterwards when it has settled down on your shoulder, a mutual confidence. It is vain of its fur, its striped paws, its ears and its whiskers, but I have never

THIS CAT SITS ON A BRICK GATE-POST, AND MEOWS TO PASSING STRANGERS TO BE NOTICED.

How Animals Study their Appearance

known a cat to be vain of its collar, though sometimes it is of a bow; a bow is a real conceit, and many of my cats know that a cat show is on for the day if they are compelled to wear a bow; sometimes they sulk and won't look up all day, but sit with drooping head. Others will choose the top of an armchair and smirk and purr with pride and content. There is no doubt about it; a bright bow will sometimes make a dirty cat wash herself clean, but the real glory of the cat is its fine whiskers; given fine whiskers you will have perfectly healthy cats.

A BOW IS A REAL CONCEIT.

Dogs have not the same vanity as a cat. A dog loves human notice. It loves to be talked to, to be called pet names. It responds to the voice, and thereby gains confidence begotten of vanity. Its vanity is such that, in the case of a pug I possessed, he would puff with pride and vain-glory with a big blue bow round his neck, while if a pink bow took its place he would wrinkle, snort and hang his tongue sulkily out of his mouth, and drag along the ground slowly. Why, I do not know, but our pug was vain of his back view and his curly tail, as he invariably looked at visitors to the house over his shoulders, while he turned his back to them. He would follow a man in the street, overtake him, and if he did not like his appearance he would, on looking up at him, drop his head, sneeze, and walk off; while if the man satisfied him, he would walk in front of him as though he wanted people to think that he was his master. The men he invariably took to wore red or orange neckties. That was his badge of gentility in others. The women who attracted him were loud of voice and diction. That was his preference!

A Japanese spaniel I possess has a great fancy for hats; if a hat is tied on his head he will show himself off in every room in the house seeking for fresh praise from every member of the family.

The same dog is vain of his eyes, and gets what he wants by opening his eyes appealingly until they are immense and round. This is especially so with the milkman, or when he wants attention and notice. "Oh, ain't he got a pair of peepers," quoth the milkman once, and since then the "pair of peepers" have hypnotised the milkman into giving short measure in order that he may give some milk to the possessor of the irresistible "peepers"!

The biggest bit of vanity, however, is left for a Chinchilla Persian. This cat sits on the brick gate-post and meows to the passing strangers to be noticed, and he is never tired of listening to the nice things they say of him.

A JAPANESE SPANIEL I POSSESS HAS A GREAT FANCY FOR HATS.

IF A PINK BOW TAKES ITS PLACE HE WILL WHIMPER AND HANG HIS TONGUE SULKILY.

Studies of Cats
From Louis Wain's Sketch-Book

IN THIS PICTURE YOU SEE PUSSY IN AN UNUSUAL SLEEPING ATTITUDE.

A COMFORTABLE SORT OF A CAT FOR THE HEARTHRUG.

TAKING THE AIR AS WELL AS FORTY WINKS.

"I HEAR THAT EARS ARE BEING WORN UPRIGHT THIS SEASON."

"WHO SAID A MOUSE?"

"YOU'LL EXCUSE MY LEAVING RATHER HURRIEDLY. I'M NOT ON SPEAKING TERMS WITH THE NEXT-DOOR DOG."

"WON'T NOBODY HELP ME?"

"I BEG PARDON! NO OFFENCE MEANT."

"I DON'T THINK THAT CANARY COULD HAVE BEEN QUITE DONE; IT DOESN'T SEEM TO HAVE AGREED WITH ME."

READY FOR A FRAY.

"TAKE THAT!"

RECKONING UP THE DAMAGES!

'A Cat Society': The World of Louis Wain's Annuals, 1901-1921

The annuals collected short stories and essays, written by some obscure and some well-known figures such as Sir William Ingram (proprietor of *The Illustrated London News* and Wain's first patron), all crammed between a prolific untidy menagerie of characteristic drawings. In their combination of eye-blinking naivety of thought and simple wacky charm they are the essence of Wain; it is the school magazine meets Pets' Corner. It is Wain's cat world: humans clad in fur but less concerned with dogs, comfort and the price of fish, and more taken up with the stylish endeavours of Edwardian England. Cats dress up to dance, to dine, to flaunt their fashionable ways, to play sports, to make music, to brush with the Law, to squabble domestically and to express strong political opinions; all a bit offbeat and foolish of course, but then the English public were prepared to laugh at themselves more easily when presented with comic social disorder out of the mouths of babes and animals.

This was the difficult annual formula that six different publishers attempted between the years 1901-15, with the ubiquitous publisher John F Shaw & Co involved in the fourteenth issue. A gap of six years intervened until the final volume appeared in 1921. These years not only cover the peak of Wain's fame, with the simultaneous production of hundreds of books and postcards, but also mark his watershed. By the time he had struggled to the outbreak of war, his business ineptitude was hampered further by his difficult personality, and a state of mind that was to slowly slide out of confident reality into disabling psychosis.

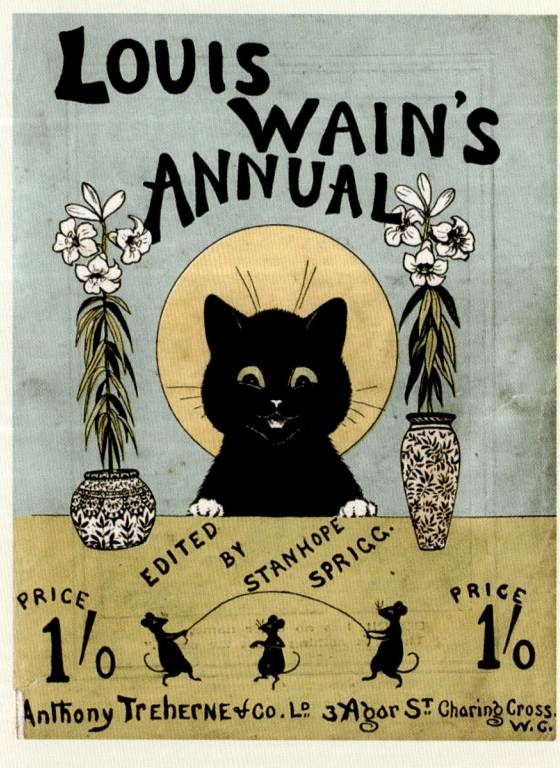

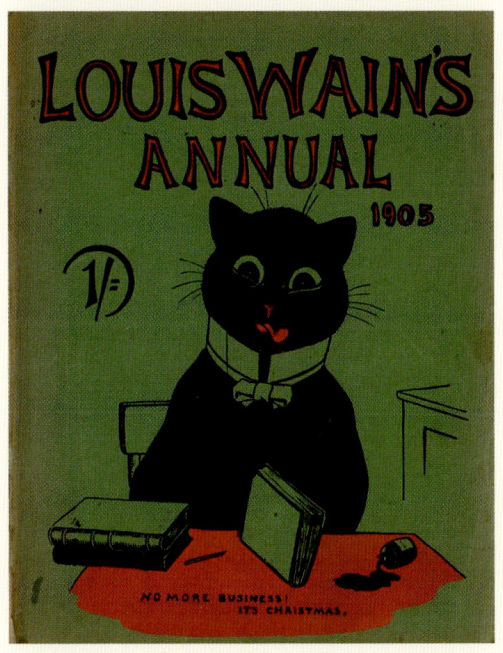

The Musical Life of Louis Wain

In all phases of Wain's career as an illustrator the theme of music resonates amusingly. We know that he played the piano and the violin and claimed skills of composition. In 1899, he recalled the days of his education in a published autobiographical fragment:

> Contact with musical people determined me to devote my future career to music, and easy going masters carried me through a lot of work; and my circumstances allowed me scope to compose a great deal, including an opera made up entirely of choruses, quartettes and duets.

Like so many amateur musicians before and since, there persists a longing for performance on the professional stage, and the approbation of artistic peers.

In 1925 Alfred Praga, a miniature painter, wrote of many evenings spent with Wain in the time of *fin de siècle* Bohemia:

> I think I first met him in Phil May's studio in the days when my studio was next door to Phil's in the Holland Park Road. In those days, Phil May's studio, on Sunday evenings, was the Mecca of all the artists and journalists of London.

> Louis Wain became a frequent visitor to my studio at the monthly musical reunions we always held when my wife was living. He was passionately fond of music – music of the elevated and classical order – and would improvise at the piano most remarkable harmonies. He claimed to have composed more than one opera, which he hoped one day to see produced.

Above: CATERWAULING
Facing page: THE ROOFTOP PARTY

Collingwood Ingram, son of Sir William Ingram, as a young man befriended the artist. He later communicated this to Rodney Dale, reliving many aspects of Wain's eccentricity:

His interest in music? Well, he used to improvise at the piano very competently, strange melodies played in a very jerky, nervous way – what I would call *agitato* playing. And he used to improvise wild, fantastic solo dances in the same style. He was quite a versatile chap.

Between clubbable Sunday evenings at Phil May's studio and genteel ensemble recitals with his talented sisters at home, Louis Wain probably kept his fingers supple; but it is in his work that he would live out a full range of vicarious musical productions such as predictable wild cat roof partying and caterwauling to vast, cacophonous bands and a satisfying apotheosis of a composer (see page 47).

Left: CAT AT A PIANO

Facing page: PIANO CAT

Above: CATERWAULING
Facing page: THE ROOFTOP PARTY

Collingwood Ingram, son of Sir William Ingram, as a young man befriended the artist. He later communicated this to Rodney Dale, reliving many aspects of Wain's eccentricity:

> His interest in music? Well, he used to improvise at the piano very competently, strange melodies played in a very jerky, nervous way – what I would call *agitato* playing. And he used to improvise wild, fantastic solo dances in the same style. He was quite a versatile chap.

Between clubbable Sunday evenings at Phil May's studio and genteel ensemble recitals with his talented sisters at home, Louis Wain probably kept his fingers supple; but it is in his work that he would live out a full range of vicarious musical productions such as predictable wild cat roof partying and caterwauling to vast, cacophonous bands and a satisfying apotheosis of a composer (see page 47).

Left: CAT AT A PIANO

Facing page: PIANO CAT

Above: CATERWAULING
Facing page: THE ROOFTOP PARTY

Collingwood Ingram, son of Sir William Ingram, as a young man befriended the artist. He later communicated this to Rodney Dale, reliving many aspects of Wain's eccentricity:

His interest in music? Well, he used to improvise at the piano very competently, strange melodies played in a very jerky, nervous way – what I would call *agitato* playing. And he used to improvise wild, fantastic solo dances in the same style. He was quite a versatile chap.

Between clubbable Sunday evenings at Phil May's studio and genteel ensemble recitals with his talented sisters at home, Louis Wain probably kept his fingers supple; but it is in his work that he would live out a full range of vicarious musical productions such as predictable wild cat roof partying and caterwauling to vast, cacophonous bands and a satisfying apotheosis of a composer (see page 47).

Left: CAT AT A PIANO

Facing page: PIANO CAT

Right: MR SCARS SINGS THE LATEST POPULAR BALLAD WHICH EVERYONE IN THE ROOM CAME TO SING

Below right: THE RECORD OF A PREVIOUS ENGAGEMENT
Published in *Louis Wain's Annual*, 1909-10

Clockwise from above left: THE VIOLINIST

MUSIC IN PUSSYTOWN (Father Tuck's 'Wonderland Series')
London: Raphael Tuck & Sons, circa 1920, front cover

I WOULD I WERE A BIRD THAT I MIGHT FLY TO THEE …

(MRS PUSSUMS) SERVE YOU RIGHT, MR PUSSUMS,
YOU SHOULDN'T HAVE SUNG THAT TOP NOTE WITH
A TREMOLO LAST NIGHT ON THE TILES

THE PIANO PLAYER

Above: THE VILLAGE BAND

Left: AND THE BAND PLAYS ON

Louis Wain on Law and Order

Louis Wain's attitude to Law and Order was predictably simplistic and would always be a forum where stereotypes of legal process and sanction were represented in harsh reality. The severe order of a courtroom is inhabited by fierce lawyers and inevitable punishment. Not for him the successful plaintiff satisfied with the benign dispensing of justice, for there in his courtroom is the end point that comes from the natural order of things. As ever in Wain's work animals as humans emphasise this ruthlessness even more pointedly; it is Victorian society red in tooth and claw. And if there is humour in it at all it lies in the gross theatricality that inhabits so much of Wain's urban society at work and at play. This is the world of Gilbert & Sullivan, of *Trial by Jury* and Ko Ko's 'little list'.

Wain's only known direct confrontation with the law was a lawsuit in 1907, which he lost, probably for the recovery from him of debt. This year of penury was shortly before, and may have contributed to, his sudden departure to work in America for Randolph Hearst.

Right: THE BARRISTER

Facing page: AND THEN THE JUSTICE ...

Above right: LAW IN ACTION

Right: THE CORONER'S COURT

Facing page: A BARRISTER'S BRIEF

The Politics of Louis Wain

MY FIRST SPEECH

Louis Wain and his Cats were Political Animals and held strong views boldly spoken. The freewheeling content of the Annuals, apparently devoid of editorial control, gave voice to some of these opinions and Wain used it like a soap box orator. Indeed the cat cartoons have all the fascination that is felt at Speakers' Corner: eccentric views, both general and obscure, mixed together and forcibly expressed to the great entertainment of everybody, none of whom has the slightest idea what he is going on about.

His cartoons seemed to mask his own views with confused and contradictory captioning, but in his letters to magazines and newspapers his optimistic views were clear enough. These show him to be a capitalist, loyalist and colonialist who believed in Free Trade. Though he expressed these views as a commentator, his political cartoons are less satire and more graphic reportage, with slight added irony at best.

THE FIRST PEACE TREATY AND WHY IT WAS NOT THE LAST
This pen and ink drawing, published in *Louis Wain's Annual* in 1905, includes an early sighting of one of his unique 'striped cats', in this case nursing a broken head in the right foreground. Despite the signing of the *Entente cordiale* the year before, the sentiments suggested here have an eerie pessimistic prognostication.

BE DAD AN' WE'LL LOVE YER!
T P O'CONNOR TO A BIRRELL: 'CHOOSE YOUR STICK AND BE ONE OF US'
This pen and ink cartoon was published in *Louis Wain's Annual* in 1907.

Thomas Power O'Connor was an influential Irish nationalist politician and respected journalist, who represented Liverpool as an MP from 1885 until his death in 1929. Augustine Birrell was Chief Secretary for Ireland from January 1907 until his resignation in 1916. These were complex and divided times in Anglo-Irish politics and Wain flags up every banner of problematical dissent. So the cat on the left holds the stick of Home Rule in his hand symbolising his attempt to get through his Irish Council Bill, while under his arm is the stick of Lord Clanricarde, the hated and cruel largest landowner in Ireland. A simultaneous bill was promised to evict the ageing and incompetent absentee landlord. T P O'Connor would famously review John D Rockefeller's book, *Random Reminiscences of Men and Events*, comparing him to Lord Clanricarde for his lack of self-reproach.

THE BANGED DOOR
Published in *Louis Wain's Annual* in 1907, this pen and ink drawing refers to the chronic problem of what the Australian Prime Minister of the time Alfred Deakin called 'the fetish of free trade'. Asquith's government of the day was strongly for free trade and resisted the Tariff Reform whereby taxes would be levied on imported goods with trade preference given to the Empire.

THE SOCIALIST'S IDEA OF A RISE IN THE WORLD
Published in *Louis Wain's Annual* in 1906, this cartoon was originally inscribed with the alternative title, 'The Boot'. Both sum up the artist's often-stated antagonism to 'Socialism'.

HOME RULE AND AFTER
MR REDMOND HAS A BAD NIGHTMARE OVER OFFICE SEEKERS
This pen and ink cartoon was published in *Louis Wain's Annual* in 1914. The Liberal Prime Minister, Herbert Asquith, had always been in support of Home Rule for Ireland, and the Third Home Rule Bill had been in discussion since 1912, with the Irish Nationalist MP and leader of the Home Rule Party preparing to compromise, so that Ulster remained Unionist in return for locally devolved powers. As civil war threatened Ireland, the enactment of the bill was overtaken by the First World War. The Easter Rising of 1916 was to prove an even bigger nightmare.

THE INSURANCE BILL
MR LLOYD GEORGE: 'HOW DO YOU LIKE YOUR NEW SUIT?'
WORKING MAN: 'BUT IT DON'T FIT.'
MR LLOYD GEORGE: 'AH, IT WILL SHRINK WITH ONE OR TWO SHOWERS!'

Produced for *Louis Wain's Annual* in 1913, this pen and ink drawing hints at a number of political events, probably in mild censure of David Lloyd George, who was then the Chancellor of the Exchequer in the Asquith Liberal administration. He had benefited from insider trading when purchasing shares in Marconi in the summer of 1912 prior to the award of a lucrative government contract. As Chancellor, his social reforms in the National Insurance Bill contained a health and unemployment insurance scheme. As Wain had a reflex hate of socialist ideals, he probably did not approve of this. However, the rampant heartless capitalism he had observed in America in the three years up to 1910 had produced feelings of compassionate ambivalence. The tailoring may be a cartoon metaphor but could indicate an anti-semitic notion rife at the time and the subject of a successful libel lawsuit; the Attorney General at the time, Sir Rufus Isaacs, was the brother of Godfrey Isaacs, Marconi's managing director.

Louis Wain's Sporting Life

Louis Wain's publications are filled with images of sporting cats reflecting the new age of leisure and organised games for the Edwardian middle classes, and of course his own predilection for hearty outdoor activities. We know much of his sporting efforts: sparring with Jem Mace the champion boxer, swimming and boating at Margate, dressing up for the local Westgate-on-Sea Tennis Club, and – as *The Idler* (see page 65) reveals – a regular jogger for the final three miles home from Margate station.

The sporting field is used by Louis Wain not so much for adulation of victory, or even triumph of the Corinthian spirit, but for the comic possibilities of trying too hard to win as his cats risk loss, climactic failure and injury on their field of dreams.

THE BOWLING MATCH

Above left: WHO'S FOR TENNIS?
Above: THE JOCKEY

Above left: AFTER THE FOOTBALL MATCH: YOU ARE NOT LUCKY, BUT A BETTER TIME IS COMING

Below left: "OH! THIS IS NOT CRICKET!"

Above right: CATS FENCING

Below right: THE SPORTSMAN: A MODERN SCHOOL OUTFIT

PREPARATION FOR
SPORTS DAY

Above left: PLAYING BALL

Above right: B. LITTLE BENJAMIN, PLAYING AT BALL: HE TOSSES, HE CATCHES, & N'ER LETS IT FALL

Below left: SNOOKER

Below right: BILLIARDS

Above left: THE DRIVE
Below left: THE GREEN
Above right: THE APPROACH
Below right: THE PUTT

Above left: SKATING ON THIN ICE

Below left: HOOKED UP

Above right: THE CATS' BOAT RACE

Below right: THE CARD PLAYERS

Facing page: CATS' BRIDGE CLUB

The Fashionable Louis Wain

In Louis Wain's Annuals there can be seen early prototypes of fashion magazines with catalogues of high and low fashion on parade. They have a celebratory attitude to the conspicuous consumption of Edwardian times, a society at play, a society at peace with itself and prepared to tolerate a little teasing for its vanity and sartorial indulgences. This display normally takes place within the marital relationship when light-hearted banter accompanies the dressing up or dressing down at the end of a hard night out.

'JOHN, WHAT ARE YOU DOING WITH MY ROUGE?'
HE (HASTILY): 'I'M MAKING UP FOR THE PART OF THE PUPPET'
Published in *Louis Wain's Annual*, in 1909-1910

OFF ON HONEYMOON

THE GENTLE WIFE
'NO SIGN OF THAT "BRIDGE" PARTY BREAKING UP YET;
MY JACK MUST BE WINNING
Published in *Louis Wain's Annual*, in 1907

What do you think of my last bargain? 5s 3/4 a yard?!

Above left: MAN AND HIS MASTER
SHE: 'WHAT AN AWFULLY PRETTY GIRL!'
HE: 'AS IN A LOOKING-GLASS, EH?'
Published in *Louis Wain's Annual*, in 1903

Above: I WILL PAY ALL YOUR LOSSES, LADY DAINTY, IF YOU INTRODUCE ME AMONG YOUR SET.

Facing page: WHAT DO YOU THINK OF MY LATEST BARGAIN? 5 ¾ A YARD!
Published in *Louis Wain's Annual*, in 1915

Above: A CHANGE! WHAT A LOVELY BRUNETTE. YES, ONE CAN SCARCELY RECOGNISE HER, SHE WAS A BLONDE SO LONG!

Above right: THERE! DID YOU EVER SEE A GIRL TURN OUT A BETTER PIECE OF WORK THAN THIS?
Published in *Louis Wain's Annual,* in 1915

Below left: DEAR ME, THIS UMBRELLA IS SO FASHIONABLE THAT I CANNOT OPEN IT IN CASE IT SPOILS THE SHAPE
Published in *Louis Wain's Annual,* in 1915

Below right: HE – I WENT TO THE ZOO YESTERDAY.
SHE – MY WORD! I WENT THERE TOO LOOKING FOR YOU.
WHICH CAGE WERE YOU IN?

OH DEAR
FRIEND: 'IT IS LIKE YOU, CERTAINLY, BADLY PAINTED.'
Published in *Louis Wain's Annual*, in 1915

MOTHER. 'HOW DID YOU GET ON THIS TERM TOMMY?'
BOY. 'OH FINE! I HAVE BEATEN ALL THE BIG BOYS, GIVEN THEM MEASLES.'
Published in *Louis Wain's Annual*, in 1915

Dining with Louis Wain

Louis Wain revealed a predilection in his Annuals for food jokes, particularly domestic humour, where another layer of jolly strife is picked over between husband and wife. The temperature of his jokey pessimism increases as he gets out of the kitchen into the world of mistrust and misfortune that is formal dining. Here waiter and consumer face off as the diner ends up the victim in a world beset by incompetent chefs cast as poisoners, or pretentious and offensive waiters serving fanciful (usually French) fare. It is a world of spiced mouse, sparrow patties and plovers on toast; and no good can come of it.

Right: THE WAITER

Facing page, clockwise from top left:
IT WASN'T MILK!

MOUSE PIE!

THAT WAS NOT A GOOD MOUSE!

HURRY UP WITH THAT DINNER PLEASE OR THE MICE JOINT WILL RUN AWAY

SPEAK, SARDINES SPEAK!
DINER: ARE THESE THE FRENCH SARDINES THAT YOU HAVE GIVEN ME,
IRISH WAITER: NOW AS IS THAT I CAN'T SAY, FOR THEY WERE
PASHT SHPAKING WHIN WE OPENED THE BOX
Published in *Louis Wain's Annual*, in 1915

In Sickness and Health with Louis Wain

Until the breakdown in Louis Wain's mental state and his incarceration, he had enjoyed robust good health and sporting fitness, and would have been unlikely to have been dependent on the medical profession. He certainly developed an irreverent attitude in his illustrative work and portrayed doctors with disapproval or at the very least mistrust. Cats' diseases and sexual abandon transferred seamlessly by implication to the world of humans and, in an age of widespread prostitution and abandoned orphans, it seems like a well-placed ironic challenge to prevailing hypocrisy.

Right: I HEAR THAT YOU SPENT YOUR VACATION AMONG FRIENDS

Facing page: A VISIT TO THE DOCTOR

Above left: THE QUACK DOCTOR
'THIS LOTION IS A POSITIVE CURE FOR SCRATCHES AND BRUISES. IT RESTORES FUR AND ALL OTHER INJURIES AFTER A FIGHT.'
Published in *Louis Wain's Annual*, in 1905

Above: ARE YOU OUR PA?

Left: 'SIMPLY MIX IT IN PIECES WITH MUSTARD PEPPER SALT & COLOURING MATTER & CALL IT JUGGED GAME AND HE'LL SWALLOW IT'

Facing page: CAT-ASTROPHE

A Postcard from Louis Wain

It is inevitable that Louis Wain would become associated with the postcard image. His rise to fame exactly overlaps the great age of the postcard from 1900-1915, and it is with this medium that public recognition fixes him forever in the collective memory of popular culture. More than a hundred publishers would distribute his 1100 images in millions of sets throughout Europe and the English-speaking world.

The humour was a more succinct version of the well-rehearsed 'cat world' of his populous prints and particularly the jokey motifs in his Annuals. Some of the most successful sets featured the situation comedy from these volumes.

It was, however, in this concentrated visual gag that he was able to present his most stylish and memorable cats. The star of many of the postcards is the cat as a wag, a joker, the stand-up comedian of the animal world (see opposite), whose social counterpart was the 'Knut', based on Phil May (1864-1903), the raffish flawed genius who dominated the bohemian artistic world in the 1890s. Louis Wain briefly immersed himself in this set and recreates the type, the model of the smartly dressed man about town never far from a pretty lady, a quip, a cigar and probably a drink too many.

This was the wide boy cat having fun at the margins of proscribed behaviour, and hence very popular for sending postal messages that a repressed society was not able to say in polite company. Wain compounded this merriment with a series of stock types on the edge of social acceptability, often making their debut in the Annuals and following up with guest appearances in the postcards. Here he would parade his stereotypes to best-selling acclaim: the inebriate, the conman, the chancer and the mountebank. Here too was the idiot victim of circumstance caught in ever bigger disasters of their own making. It was Catland's version of Laurel and Hardy and the Keystone Cops. Here too was the vicarious delight in the instability of other people's marriages. For a man but briefly married and thereafter enclosed by suffocating sisterhood, his domestic material affords insightful humour with scenes of incomprehension, tension and petty violence as cats mimic the excesses of matrimonial bliss: the tardy homecoming drunk, the hen-pecked husband, the profligate wife, and the chores of child-minding.

There are many prototypes or trial runs in his books, annuals and series of prints that appear again in the more portable postcard form later. These succinct narratives or striking singular images probably contributed more to Louis Wain's fame and penetration of the Edwardian era than any other and, though produced in their millions at the time, enough have survived obsolescence to enchant succeeding generations of collectors. The reference bible of these collectors is likely to be an enjoyable paperback brought out in 1985 by two American postcard devotees, Cynthia Delulio and Elsa Ross. *Especially Cats. Louis Wain's Humorous Postcards* is impressively compiled and has all the obsessive detail and opinion you would expect from true enthusiasts.

It is easy to share their praise for a particular postcard type, the mascot cat. Here the cats, and occasionally dogs, developed a squat angular almost cuboid shape and this jolly morphology seemed to give Wain another expressive option for his catty types. The mascot animals in the final famous postcard series published by Raphael Tuck in 1931 have earlier antecedents. In *Louis Wain's Annual* of 1903, cats appeared as 'microbes' (see page 142) and at this period Max Ettlinger & Co published a set of six postcards of these chunky cats in threes. By the time the Philco Publishing Co brought out another set of stylised sporting threesomes, in 1908, the look was fixed (see page 143).

THE CHAIRMAN'S CIGAR

Left: MORE CAT MICROBES
Published in *Louis Wain's Annual*, in 1903

Facing page: WE'RE THINKING OF DROPPING THIS AND GOING IN FOR LIMERICKS
(Delulio & Ross, page 107)
The surreal title given to this postcard does not really sound like Louis Wain's wit but this sanguine view of the sporting world accords with his routines of danger and damage.

Below: STAGE DOOR JOHNNIES
Chunky mascot cats became more refined as Wain used them more in his society tableaux, as in this charming artwork which is known to have been left in his estate.

Clockwise from top left:

HAPPY KITTEN
This is a prototype for the dumpty mascot cat.

CAT IN A STIFF COLLAR
The prototype cat stands and is clothed; evolution is complete.

VANITY SPOILS HIS CHANCE
Wain adds a title that is suitably stretching and strange.

THE NEW HOUSEMAID
Domesticity is never easy in Catland.

Above left: THE SKIPPING MASCOT

Above right: THE CONTENTED MASCOT

Left: THE HUNTSMAN'S MASCOT

The three pleasingly silly pictures on this page were produced for Raphael Tuck & Sons and published by them in four series of postcards from about 1931.

Clockwise from top left:

A STRIPED CATS' CHORUS

THE PRIMA DONNA OF THE NIGHT

STRIPED CATS
Striped cats rank with Mascot cats as Wain 'pedigrees' of capricious cheer and inventive flair. They also had their genesis in the early days of the Annuals and were perfected later to star in postcards by Raphael Tuck in their 'Stripes to the Front' series in about 1916, and in a series by Solomon Brothers in 1914, where patriotic World War One soldier cats wear their amended stripes in Union Jack motifs.

Clockwise from top:

MATRIMONIAL DIFFERENCES
A design for a postcard published by J Beagles & Co, 1908, in a series of married twosomes with beguiling titles of eternal truth: *I Love You*, *Scandal*, *Peacemaker*, *The Tiff* and *Reconciliation*.

ONE OVER THE EIGHT OR THAT CAT AGAIN
This cheerful reprobate cat from *Louis Wain's Annual* of 1908 appears again and again in books and in postcard series, accompanied by minor variations in inebriate ataxia and titles such as *Who Shaid P-Pusshy Foot* (Valentines & Sons) and *And It Wasn't Milk* (J Beagles & Co).

WHAT TIME DO YOU CALL THIS? KISS-MISS TIME MY DEAR

Above: AT FIRST, THE INFANT, MEWLING AND PEWKING IN THE NURSE'S ARMS, OR SATURDAY NIGHT

Below: AND THEN, THE LOVER, SIGHING LIKE FURNACE, WITH A WOEFUL BALLAD MADE TO HIS MISTRESS' EYEBROW
These two pictures and the *The Night Attack* on page 88 were painted for 'The Seven Ages' series of postcards based on Jacques' speech in Shakespeare's *As You Like It*.

149

Above: WAITING THEIR TURN
Design for a postcard for Valentines & Sons, unnumbered series (h), 'Seaside Activities', circa 1908

Postcards of Edwardian society at play demonstrating their new-found freedoms to travel by rail to the seaside were ever popular, and Wain gave it his usual manic populous flavour, as these two designs and the picture on the dust jacket of this book demonstrate.

Left: THE RAILWAY STATION, HOLIDAY TIME

Above left: A TALE OF WOE
From Raphael Tuck's the 'Nursery' series published in 1920

Above right: THE ONE THAT GOT AWAY
The theme of the cat as a failed hunter recurs in many variations in Wain's work, with titles like *The One that Got Away, You Naughty Bird,* or most wittily *And The Doctor Said I Must Not Move,* as a cat isolated in bed with toothache confronts a cheeky bird just out of reach. The situation comedy of violent symbiosis is years ahead of Tom and Jerry.

Facing page (clockwise from top left): The most popular of all the postcard series, however, showed cats that were beautiful: portrait cats, handsome cats, flirty cats, vain cats, society cats, popularly in threes but singular cats all.

THREE'S COMPANY

THREE'S A CROWD

GINGER TOM

GEISHA CAT

The Late Work of Louis Wain

'There are people who love nature even though they are cracked and ill, those are the painters.'

— Vincent Van Gogh

This remarkable body of imagery, structurally complex but instantly pleasurable, was produced late in Louis Wain's life, during his hospital years and largely outside of commercial pressures. I believe that it can be confronted with all its vibrancy and intensity, but still be viewed with simple delight. Indeed it can be taken in three times a day and without medical supervision. It can be judged merely by its aesthetics, rather than analysed as a manifestation of inner feelings and distorted observations: a pictorial expression of inner disorders of perception. The pleasures of an ice cream on a hot summer's day are not enhanced by enquiry into its constituent e-numbers.

So much of the comment on schizophrenic art is at present only conjecture and, in Wain's case, plainly wrong. The well-rehearsed discussions surrounding the over-scrutinised schizophrenic imagery in the admirable Guttman-Maclay collection in the Bethlem Royal Hospital Archive and Museum will attest to this pseudo-scientific approach. From 1924 until his death 15 years later, Wain was in a period of artistic repose where asylum gave him the freedom from

demands, deadline and debt, and here he found something of his true practice. Here style and content often combine with just the right weight of colour and form to produce works of sensuous beauty. They do not require explanatory narrative or a need for placement in a familiar world. So this kaleidoscopic queue of urgent bright images is presented as such in this last chapter, and a title is ascribed only when it is known to have originated from the artist at the time.

Facing page: SWEET SCENTED

Above right: THE PURPLE HERON FROM THE HIGH MOUNTAINS

Above right: THE SPANISH GONDOLIERS

Above: DADDY CAN YOU LET ME PASS ON
YOUR LOVE TO MOTHER FROM ME

Facing page, far right: EARLY GREEK

Facing page, far right: EARLY GREEK

EARLY SPANIOL

Above left: MAARISH

Facing page: THE EARLY INDIAN IRISH

Above: OUR ENTERTAINER

Above: THE EARLY ITALIAN

Above left: EARLY GREEK

Louis Wain Lucky Futurist Mascots
An Introduction

David Wootton

It is now widely accepted that the work of Louis Wain comprises one of the most distinctive and enduring achievements of Edwardian popular art. Nevertheless, the series of 20 ceramic 'mascot' animals that he launched in 1914 remains one of the most original and startling products of his career. This is not just because these ceramics are his only significant three-dimensional designs to reach production, but also because they represent his most conscious response to the avant-garde artistic movements of the early twentieth century.

Between his return from America in 1910 and the appearance of his ceramics in 1914, Wain would have been able to see a number of groundbreaking exhibitions. Prominent among these were the 'Exhibition of Works by the Italian Futurist Painters' at the Sackville Gallery and the 'Second Post-Impressionist Exhibition' at the Grafton Galleries (including examples of Cubism by Braque and Picasso) – both held in London in 1912. And, even if he didn't actually see these shows himself, he would surely have followed the coverage of them in the periodical press of the time.

It is not known whether the ceramics were instigated by Wain or commissioned by Max Emanuel, the importer and retailer of glass and porcelain, who effected their production and promotion. While Emanuel was undoubtedly an entrepreneur, Wain himself was not without enterprise, as is evidenced by his earlier attempts to patent inventions. So the ceramics may have arisen from an opportunity to capitalise on the notoriety of the avant-garde artists or from a desire to parody their styles. For many of the designs suggest the forms of Cubism, the colours of Fauvism, the confident attitude of Futurism – and even touches of the more-established Japonism – while remaining true to Wain's vivid imagination.

Max Emanuel & Company was based at 41-42 Shoe Lane, near Holborn, in London. However, Emanuel owned the Mosaic Pottery in Mitterteich, Bavaria, Germany (1895-1917), and worked with many other companies, including Riessner, Stellmacher & Keppel (Amphora), based in Turn-Teplitz, Bohemia, Austria-Hungary. It is almost certain that it is the Amphora Works Riessner – a later incarnation of this Bohemian company – that produced most of Wain's larger ceramics, both before and after the First World War. The earlier examples carry the stamp 'Imperial Amphora, Austria', the later ones 'Amphora, Made in Czecho-Slovakia'. This distinction indicates the change of political identity in 1918 (the dissolution of Austria-Hungary and independence of Czechoslovakia) rather than a move for the factory. The Czech name for the town is Teplice-Trnovany.

The remainder of the, mainly small, Wain-Emanuel ceramics were, according to a stamp, 'Made in England', though at an, as yet, unidentified factory.

The other stamp to appear regularly on the earlier ceramics is that which identified Max Emanuel himself: three rifles stacked against each other to form a pyramid or, perhaps, a simplified 'M' standing for Max, Mosanic and/or Mitterteich.

On 18 May 1914, Max Emanuel registered the first of the ceramic animals with the Patent Office, under the designation 'china ornaments'. All ten [nos 1-10] were cats. However, one – *The Lucky Road Hog Cat* [no 7] – was originally described as a 'Teddy Bear', and indeed has the look of such a toy, which itself was still a novelty, having been created only a decade before by Morris Michtom of Brooklyn.

A further nine small-scale ceramics [nos 11-19] were registered on 12 June 1914. Six of these were cats, two were pigs [nos 18-19] and one a dog [no 14].

Max Emanuel launched all 19 designs at his Shoe Lane showroom on the same day – 12 June 1914 – having sent out an invitation with the motto 'Bring your smile with you, for good luck awaits you when you see us!' The one newspaper to cover this event – the *Daily Express* – reproduced a photograph of Wain in the act of painting a panel that explains the ceramics. At some point, the artist also prepared a poster (above), which he inscribed, somewhat optimistically, 'The Louis Wain Futurist Mascot Cats, bulldog & pig in porcelain china now being sold in every country and all the principle shops in Great Britain'.

As can be seen from the following catalogue, some of the larger ceramics were produced in a choice of at least as many as five colours [nos 8 & 10], and the *Daily Express* reviewer enthused about 'yellow

UNEXECUTED DESIGN FOR A SQUARE JUG

cats and blue cats, green cats and pink cats, and even pale heliotrope cats'. Furthermore, a single design was sometimes produced with variants, and probably from a range of moulds, as is indicated by discrepancies in size and finish. Most are impressed with the artist's signature and some with the ceramic's title. In addition, all may originally have had a charm attached to them, printed on a piece of paper. Fragile and detachable, few of the charms remain intact. The reviewer stated that the ceramics 'are meant for mascots', but some are shaped like vases, the smaller ones being appropriate for 'spills' – wooden sticks used to light lamps and candles. Wain had introduced the idea of the solid, defined mascot form in books from about 1910 and would return to it occasionally until a series of postcards in about 1931.

Max Emanuel registered a further of Wain's ceramics as 'China Ashtray' [no 20] on 16 November 1914, three months after the United Kingdom entered the First World War. This action may suggest that, despite the uncertain political situation, the earlier ceramics had had a degree of success, though no sales records have yet come to light.

Rodney Dale records that 'a ship carrying a cargo' of these ceramics, probably from England to America, 'was torpedoed' during the war (Dale 2000, page 79). But he admits that he has 'not been able to find out anything about the ship', and neither have I. The story tends to be cited as evidence of the ceramics' scarcity, but it also acts as a reminder of their import and export.

Production began again at the end of the First World War. Registration was extended on most of the smaller, English-made ceramics on 11 August 1919 [nos 11-13 and 15-19]. However, according to Cork Marcheschi (Marcheschi 2008, unpaginated), later examples do not carry Emanuel's triple-rifle stamp, though some have, what he calls, 'an uncommon stamped signature' and also stamped titles [eg no 18]. He speculates that 'Max Emanuel was not the agent to sell the pieces, or some of the figures were licensed to other retail outlets'.

Marcheschi's assessment of the later examples of the larger, Amphora-made ceramics is even more intriguing. Though they

UNEXECUTED DESIGN FOR A CIRCULAR JUG

'commonly' have white glazes, some are made from 'slightly different' moulds. A number have earlier manufacturing marks that 'have been intentionally blocked out', while at least one cat has a 'Fireside' importation mark [no 1]. He suggests the blacking out may be due to 'the exclusion of Austria from the Versailles Treaty'.

Marcheschi believes that 'the impetus for the 1919-22 run of cats' was the creation, in 1919, of the internationally popular American cartoon character, Felix the Cat. However, examples of only three of the many larger white cats have a 'Felix' mark [nos 7, 8 & 10], which suggests rather that it was an additional way of marketing them.

Marcheschi also touches on the subject of fakes, partly in response to the plethora of moulds, glazes and stamps. Two Wain ceramics were withdrawn from an auction at Bonhams that was due to take place on 23 and 24 September 2008. They were examples of the small version of *The Lucky Futurist Cat and his meow meow notes* [no 9] and *The Happy Jappy Cat* [no 13]. Indeed, the colour image of the latter that is included in this catalogue is of that faked example. However, that particular ceramic is so rare that there is an image of only one other example (and that a small black and white photograph in Dale 1968, page 113).

This catalogue closes with a ceramic cat that, though impressed with a Louis Wain signature, stands apart from the Lucky Futurist Mascots. It is more conventionally naturalistic, rounded and 'sweet'. Registered by – the as yet unidentified – Sidney George Parker-Fox of 24 Charlwood Street, Pimlico, London, it was manufactured by the 'Royal Staffordshire Pottery Wilkinson Ltd England'. There are examples with a bow tie other than yellow (ie blue, green and red), though they may have been overpainted at a later date.

The catalogue lists the ceramics chronologically, and then by registration number. Official titles, as impressed on the ceramic or referred to at the time, are in **bold**. The remaining are given their now common titles in [square brackets]. Exact marks, as seen, are presented in 'single inverted commas'.

References

Bamfords 2009
  Appeared in an auction at Bamfords, Derby, on 9 June 2009

Bonhams 2008
  Withdrawn from an auction at Bonhams, London, 23-24 September 2008

Chasen 2009
  'An interview with George Hochen about collecting Wain cats', blogchasenantiques.com, 1 September 2009

Chris Beetles Ltd
  As the leading dealer in Louis Wain, Chris Beetles has sold a number of the ceramics

Dale 1968
  Rodney Dale, *Louis Wain. The Man Who Drew Cats*, London: William Kimber, 1968

Dale 2000
  Rodney Dale, *Louis Wain. The Man Who Drew Cats*, London: Chris Beetles Ltd, 2000

Marcheschi 2008
  Cork Marcheschi, *Louis Wain. Lucky Futurist Mascot Cats*, Blurb.com, 2008

Martin
  Tracy Martin, 'Louis Wain & His Cats', www.worldcollectorsnet.com/magazine/issue46

Omega
  www.titusomega.com

Rago Arts 2010
  Appeared in an auction at Rago Arts, Lambertville, NJ, in April 2010

UK Private Collection
  This is one of the largest and most comprehensive collections of Louis Wain ceramics, and we are very grateful to its owners for allowing us to photograph its contents and for sharing their expertise

Proudlove
  Christopher Proudlove, 'Louis Wain's lucky pot cats now coveted collectors' items', writeantiques.com

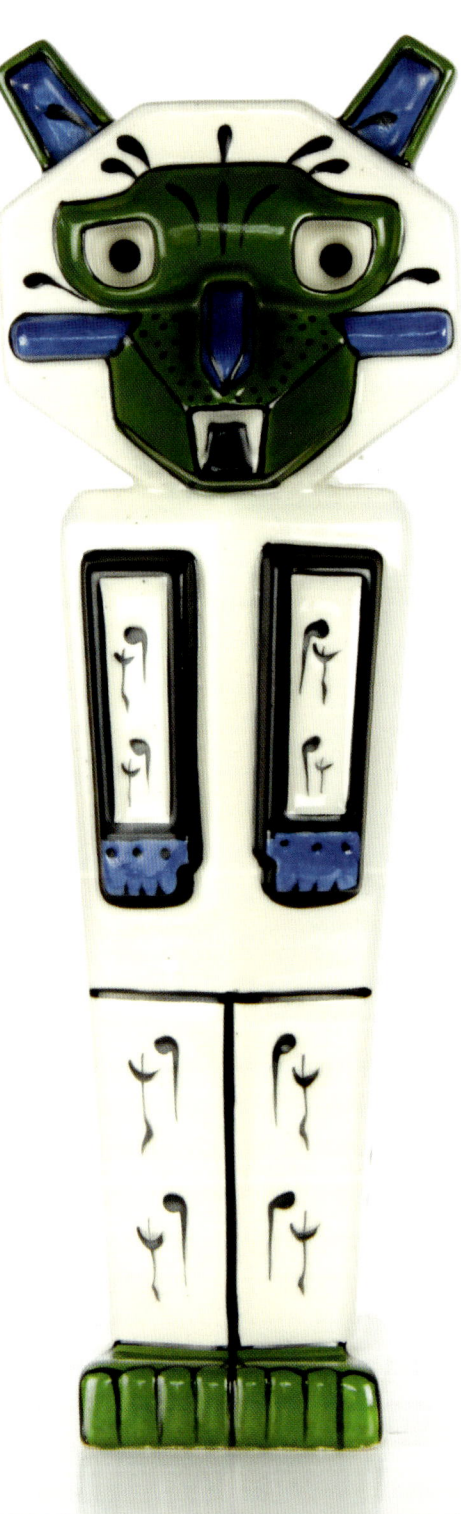

1.ii

Louis Wain Lucky Futurist Mascots
A Catalogue Raisonné
Compiled by David Wootton

1. THE LUCKY MASCOT CAT
Registered by Max Emanuel & Company,
41-42 Shoe Lane, London EC,
China Manufacturers
Reg date: 18.5.1914
Reg no: BT52/629/637127
Reg name: 'China Ornament'
Casts and glazes:
i. Unspecified colour, other than white
    (Ref: black and white photograph
    attached to the original registration
    form)

ii. White (with blue and green detailing)
    1919-22 (according to Marcheschi
    2008)
    Stamps: 'Amphora, Made in Czecho-
    Slovakia'; 'Fireside'
    Some marks have been intentionally
    blacked out
    11 inches high, 3 ¾ inches wide
    (Ref: UK Private Collection)

2. THE LUCKY SPHINX CAT
Registered by Max Emanuel & Company,
41-42 Shoe Lane, London EC,
China Manufacturers
Reg date: 18.5.1914
Reg no: BT52/629/637128
Reg name: 'China Ornament'
Casts and glazes:
i. Red (with green detailing)
    Stamps: 'Made in England'; Max
    Emanuel (3 rifles stacked against each
    other to form a pyramid)
    Painted impressed signature: 'Louis
    Wain'
    Impressed: 'Reg No 637128'
    9 ¾ inches high, 6 inches wide
    (Ref: UK Private Collection)

1.ii

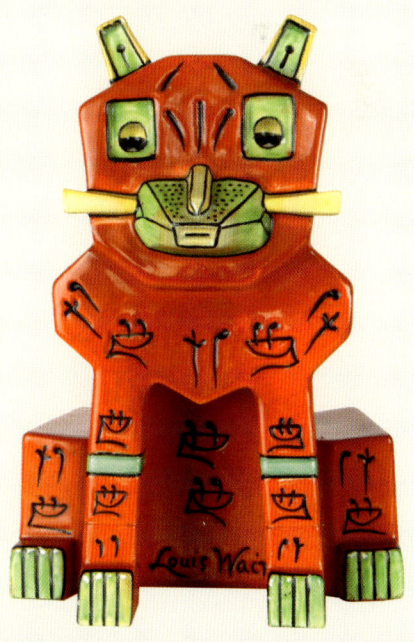

2.i

ii. Red (with green detailing)
   Stamps: Imperial Amphora, Austria; Max Emanuel
   (Ref: Marcheschi 2008)
iii. Purple (with green and orange detailing)
   Stamps: Imperial Amphora, Austria; Max Emanuel
   Impressed title: 'Lucky Sp[h]inx Cat'
   (Ref: Omega)
iv. White (with pale blue and green detailing)
   1919-22 (according to Marcheschi 2008)
   Stamp: 'Amphora, Made in Czecho-Slovakia'
   Impressed signature: 'Louis Wain'
   9 ¾ inches high, 6 inches wide
   (Ref: UK Private Collection)
v. White (with green and dark red detailing)
   1919-22 (according to Marcheschi 2008)
   Impressed signature: 'Louis Wain'
   Some marks have been intentionally blacked out
   9 ¾ inches high, 6 inches wide
   (Ref: UK Private Collection)
vi. White (with green and pale red detailing)
   1919-22 (according to Marcheschi 2008)
   (Ref: Marcheschi 2008)
vii. White (with blue detailing: the oriental blue & white look)
   1919-22 (according to Marcheschi 2008)
   (Ref: Marcheschi 2008)

3. [LARGE CAT]
Registered by Max Emanuel & Company, 41-42 Shoe Lane, London EC, China Manufacturers
Reg date: 18.5.1914
Reg no: BT52/629/637129
Reg name: 'China Ornament'
Casts and glazes:
i. Blue (with red and yellow detailing)
   Stamps: 'Made in England'; Max Emanuel
   Painted impressed signature: 'Louis Wain'
   9 ½ inches high, 8 inches long
   (Ref: UK Private Collection)

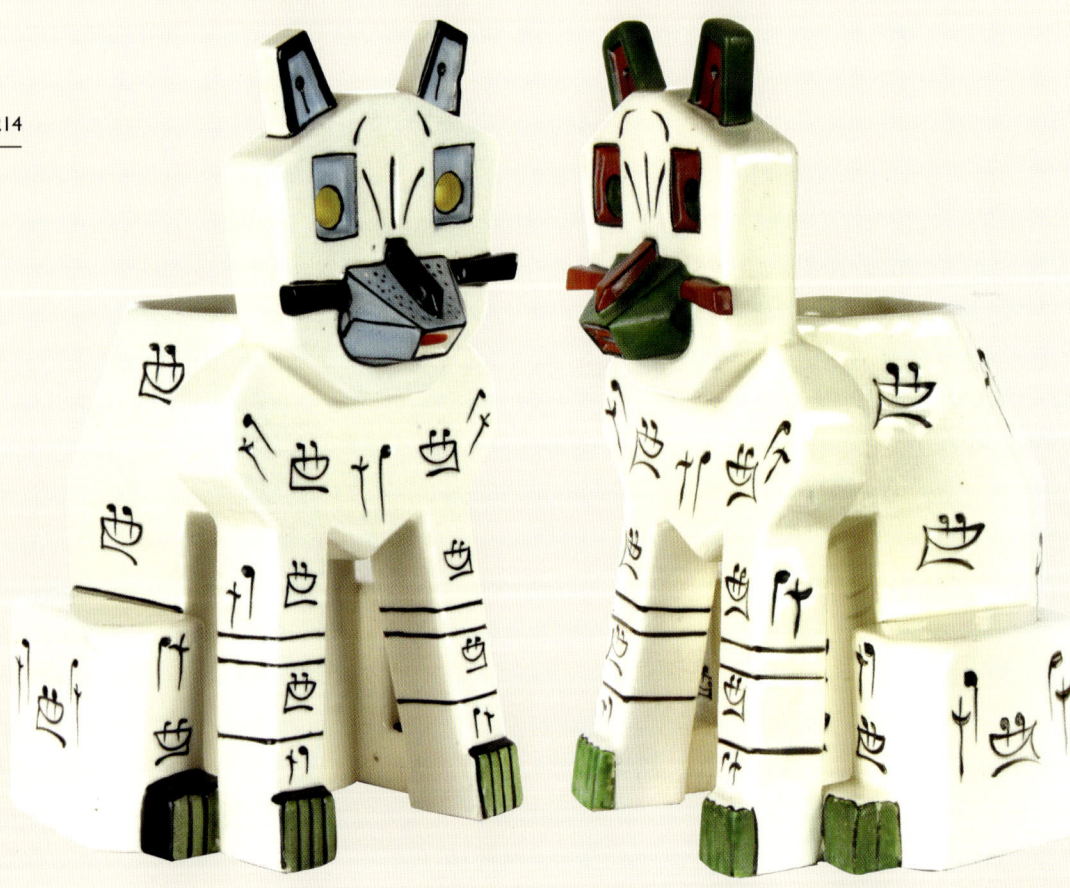

2.iv   2.v

3.i

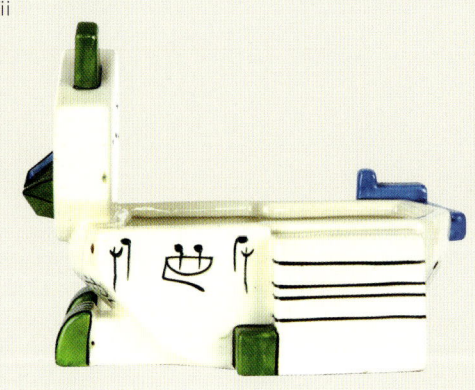

4.i

4.iii

5.i

4. THE LUCKY BOWL CAT

Registered by Max Emanuel & Company,
41-42 Shoe Lane, London EC,
China Manufacturers
Reg date: 18.5.1914
Reg no: BT52/629/637130
Reg name: 'China Ornament'
Casts and glazes:

i. Purple (with green and red detailing)
   Stamps: 'Imperial Amphora, Austria';
   Max Emanuel
   Painted impressed signature: 'Louis Wain'
   Impressed title: 'Bowl Cat'
   6 inches high, 8 inches long
   (Ref: UK Private Collection)

ii. Green (with purple and red detailing)
    Stamps: 'Imperial Amphora'; Max Emanuel
    Painted impressed signature: 'Louis Wain'
    Impressed title: 'Bowl Cat'
    6 inches high, 8 inches long
    (Ref: UK Private Collection)

iii White (with blue and green detailing)
    1919-22 (according to Marcheschi)
    Impressed signature: 'Louis Wain'
    Impressed title: 'Bowl Cat'
    Some marks have been intentionally blacked out
    6 inches high, 8 inches long
    (Ref: UK Private Collection)

4.ii

5. THE LUCKY MASTER CAT

Registered by Max Emanuel & Company,
41-42 Shoe Lane, London EC,
China Manufacturers
Reg date: 18.5.1914
Reg no: BT52/629/637131
Reg name: 'China Ornament'
(For the original design for The Lucky Master Cat, see page 76)
Casts and glazes:

i. Green (with red and yellow detailing)
   Stamps: 'Made in England'; Max Emanuel
   Painted impressed signature: 'Louis Wain'
   Impressed title: 'The Lucky Master Cat'
   Impressed: 'Reg No 637131'
   8 inches high, 7 inches long
   (Ref: UK Private Collection)

ii. Yellow (with purple and red detailing)
    Stamps: 'Imperial Amphora'; 'Austria'; Max Emanuel
    Painted impressed signature: 'Louis Wain'
    Impressed title: 'The Lucky Master Cat'
    8 inches high, 7 inches long

5.ii 5.iii

(Ref: UK Private Collection)

iii. Purple (with green and red detailing)
Painted impressed signature: 'Louis Wain'
Impressed title: 'The Lucky Master Cat'
8 inches high, 7 inches long
(Ref: UK Private Collection)

iv. Orange (with green and yellow detailing)
Stamps: Imperial Amphora, Austria; Max Emanuel
8 inches high, 7 inches long
(Ref: Marcheschi 2008)

v. White (with orange and red detailing)
1919-22 (according to Marcheschi 2008)
Impressed signature: 'Louis Wain'
Impressed title: 'The Lucky Master Cat'
8 inches high, 7 inches long
(Ref: UK Private Collection)

vi. White (with green and red detailing)
1919-22 (according to Marcheschi 2008)
Impressed title: 'The Lucky Master Cat'
(Ref: Marcheschi 2008)

5.v

6. THE FUTURIST CAT

Registered by Max Emanuel & Company,
41-42 Shoe Lane, London EC,
China Manufacturers
Reg date: 18.5.1914
Reg no: BT52/629/637132
Reg name: 'China Ornament'
Casts and glazes:

i. Blue (with red and yellow detailing)
   Stamps: Imperial Amphora, Austria; Max Emanuel
   Painted impressed signature: 'Louis Wain'
   Impressed title: 'Futurist Cat'
   10 ½ inches high, 9 ¼ inches long
   (Ref: Marcheschi 2008)

ii. Navy (with green and orange detailing)
    Stamps: 'Imperial Amphora, Austria'; Max Emanuel
    Painted impressed signature: 'Louis Wain'
    Impressed title: 'Futurist Cat'
    11 inches high, 9 ¾ inches long
    (Ref: Rago Arts 2010)

iii. Purple (with green and orange detailing)
     Stamps: Imperial Amphora, Austria; Max Emanuel
     Impressed signature: 'Louis Wain'
     10 ½ inches high, 9 ¼ inches long
     (Ref: Omega)

iv. White (with black detailing)
    1919-22 (according to Marcheschi 2008)
    Stamps: 'Imperial Amphora'; 'Austria'; Max Emanuel
    Impressed signature: 'Louis Wain'
    Impressed title: 'Futurist Cat'
    10 ½ inches high, 9 ¼ inches long
    (Ref: UK Private Collection)

v. White (with blue and red detailing)
   1919-22 (according to Marcheschi 2008)
   Stamp: 'Amphora, Made in Czecho-Slovakia'
   Impressed signature: 'Louis Wain'
   Impressed title: 'Futurist Cat'
   10 ½ inches high, 9 ¼ inches long
   (Ref: UK Private Collection)

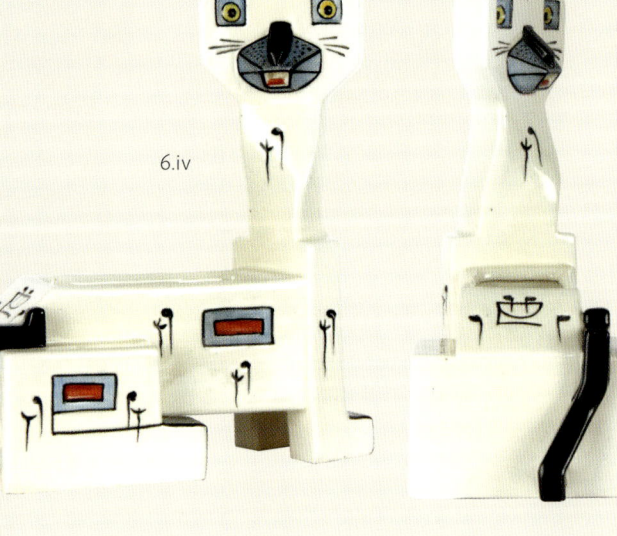

6.iv

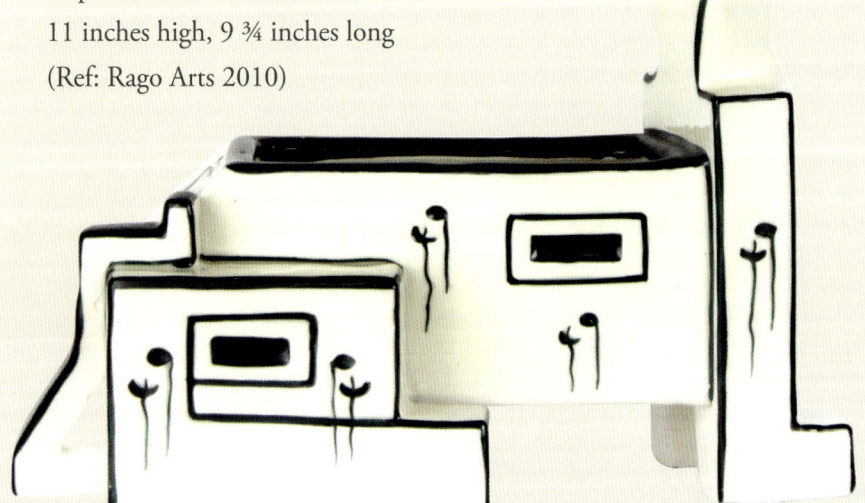

6.iii

7. THE LUCKY ROAD HOG CAT

Registered by Max Emanuel & Company,
41-42 Shoe Lane, London EC,
China Manufacturers
Reg date: 18.5.1914
Reg no: BT52/629/637133
Reg name: 'Teddy Bear' and then 'China Ornament'
Charm: 'I will drive you to good fortune. Take it and make the most of it'
Casts and glazes:

i. Pale purple (with orange and yellow detailing)
   Stamps: 'Made in England'; Max Emanuel
   Painted impressed signature: 'Louis Wain'
   8 inches high, 8 ¾ inches wide
   (Ref: Marcheschi 2008)

ii. Pale blue head, mid blue body (with red and yellow detailing)
    Stamps: Made in England; Max Emanuel
    Painted impressed signature: 'Louis Wain'
    8 inches high, 8 ¾ inches wide
    (Ref: Proudlove)

iii. Orange (with green and purple detailing)
     Stamps: 'Imperial Amphora'; 'Austria'; Max Emanuel
     Impressed signature: 'Louis Wain'
     8 inches high, 8 ¾ inches wide
     (Ref: UK Private Collection)

iv. White (with black, orange, purple and yellow detailing)
    1919-22 (according to Marcheschi 2008)
    Stamp: 'Amphora, Made in Czecho-Slovakia'
    Painted inscription: 'Felix'
    Impressed title: 'Lucky Road Hog Cat'
    (Ref: Marcheschi 2008)

v. White (with red and yellow detailing)
   1919-22 (according to Marcheschi 2008)
   Stamp: 'Amphora, Made in Czecho-Slovakia'
   Impressed title: 'The Road Hog Cat'
   8 inches high
   (Ref: Omega)

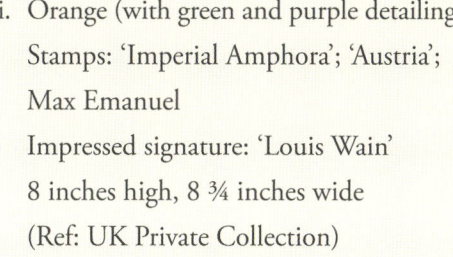

7.iii

8. THE LUCKY FUTURIST CAT AND HIS MEOW MEOW NOTES

[LARGE]

Registered by Max Emanuel & Company, 41-42 Shoe Lane, London EC, China Manufacturers

Reg date: 18.5.1914

Reg no: BT52/629/637134

Reg name: 'China Ornament'

Charm: 'Bring your smile with you, for good luck awaits you when you see me'

Casts and glazes:

i. Red (with green and yellow detailing)
   Stamp: Max Emanuel
   Painted signature: 'Louis Wain'
   Impressed title: 'Futurist Cat'
   Impressed: 'Made in England'; '63713'
   9 ¾ inches high, 6 ¾ inches long
   (Ref: UK Private Collection)

ii. Red (with green and yellow detailing)
    Stamps: Imperial Amphora, Austria; Max Emanuel
    Painted impressed signature: 'Louis Wain'
    9 ¾ inches high, 6 ¾ inches long
    (Ref: Marcheschi 2008)

iii. Blue (with red and yellow detailing)
     Stamps: Imperial Amphora, Austria; Max Emanuel
     Painted impressed signature: 'Louis Wain'
     9 ¾ inches high, 6 ¾ inches long
     (Ref: Marcheschi 2008)

8.i

iv. Purple (with pale purple detailing)
   Stamps: Imperial Amphora, Austria; Max Emanuel
   Painted signature: 'Louis Wain'
   9 ¾ inches high, 6 ¾ inches long
   (Ref: Marcheschi 2008)

v. Green (with red and yellow detailing)
   Painted impressed signature: 'Louis Wain'
   9 ¾ inches high, 6 ¾ inches long
   (Ref: Chasen 2009)

vi. White (with black, green and red detailing)
   1919-22 (according to Marcheschi 2008)
   Stamp: 'Amphora, Made in Czecho-Slovakia'
   Painted inscription: 'Felix'
   Impressed signature: 'Louis Wain'
   Impressed title: 'Futurist Cat'
   9 ½ inches high, 6 ¾ inches long
   (Ref: UK Private Collection)

vii. White (with green and pink detailing), in a much finer glaze
   1919-22 (according to Marcheschi 2008)
   Stamp: 'Amphora, Made in Czecho-Slovakia'
   Impressed title: 'Futurist Cat'
   9 ¼ inches high, 6 ½ inches long
   (Ref: UK Private Collection)

8.vi

8.vii

9. THE LUCKY FUTURIST CAT AND HIS MEOW MEOW NOTES
[SMALL]
Registered by Max Emanuel & Company, 41-42 Shoe Lane, London EC, China Manufacturers
Reg date: 18.5.1914
Reg no: BT52/629/637134
Reg name: 'China Ornament'
Charm: 'Bring your smile with you, for good luck awaits you when you see me'
Casts and glazes:
i. Green (with black, purple, red and yellow detailing)
   Stamp: Max Emanuel
   Painted signature: 'Louis Wain'
   Impressed: 'Made in England'; 'RONO 637134'
   5 ½ inches high, 3 ¼ inches long
   (UK Private Collection)

10. THE LUCKY MASTER CAT
[LARGE]
Registered by Max Emanuel & Company, 41-42 Shoe Lane, London EC, China Manufacturers
Reg date: 18.5.1914
Reg no: BT52/629/637135
Reg name: 'China Ornament'
Charm: 'Possess me and be happy'
Casts and glazes:
i. Purple (with green and red detailing)
   Stamps: Made in England; Max Emanuel
   Painted impressed signature: 'Louis Wain'
   11 ¼ inches high, 7 ½ inches long
   (Ref: Marcheschi 2008)
ii. Black (with red and yellow detailing)
    Stamps: 'Made in England'; Max Emanuel
    Painted impressed signature: Louis Wain
    11 ¼ inches high, 7 ½ inches long
    (Ref: UK Private Collection)
iii. Pale Blue (with red and yellow detailing)
     Stamps: Made in England; Max Emanuel
     Painted impressed signature: 'Louis Wain'
     11 ¼ inches high, 7 ½ inches long
     (Ref: Martin)
iv. Mid Blue (with red and yellow detailing)

9.i

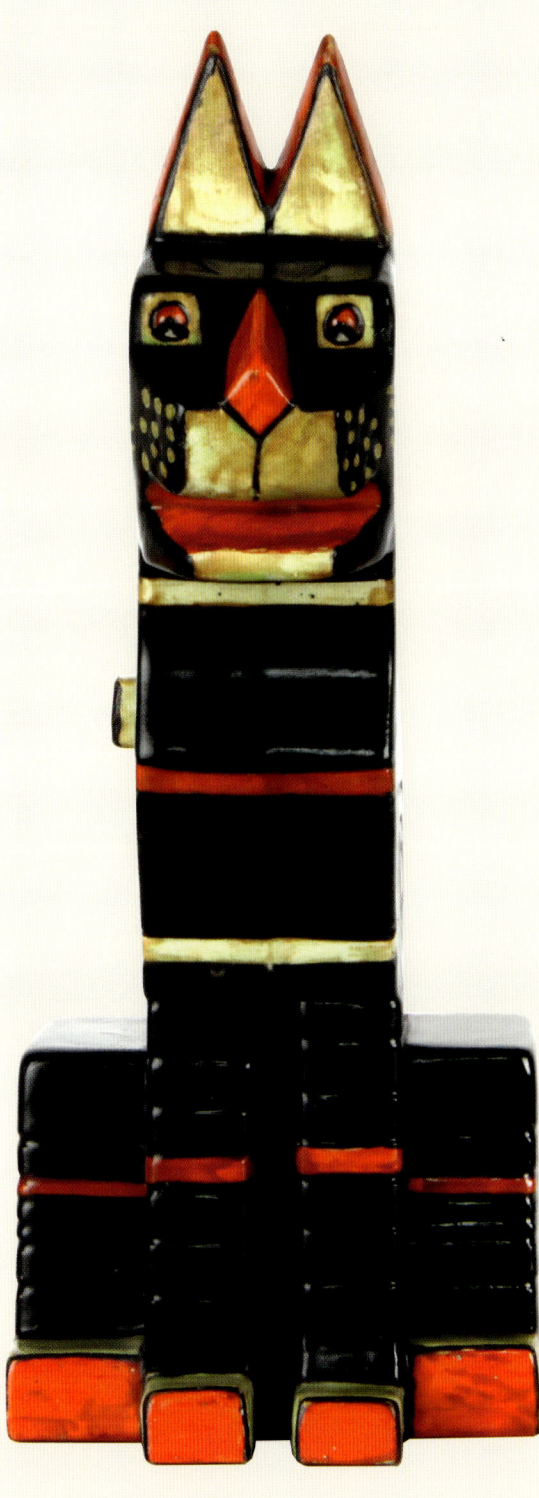

10.ii

10.v

Painted impressed signature: 'Louis Wain'
11 ¼ inches high, 7 ½ inches long
(Bamfords 2009)

v. Yellow (with blue and red detailing)
Stamps: 'Austria'; Max Emanuel
Impressed signature: 'Louis Wain'
Impressed title: 'The Futurist Cat'
11 inches high, 7 ¼ inches long
(Ref: UK Private Collection)

vi. White (with green and red detailing)
1919-22 (according to Marcheschi 2008)
Stamp: 'Amphora, Made in Czecho-Slovakia'
Impressed signature: 'Louis Wain'
Impressed title: 'The Futurist Cat'
Some marks have been intentionally blacked out
11 inches high, 7 ¼ inches long
(Ref: UK Private Collection)

vii. White (with black, purple, red and yellow detailing; black ears)
1919-22 (according to Marcheschi 2008)
Stamp: 'Amphora, Made in Czecho-Slovakia'
Painted inscription: 'Felix'
11 inches high, 7 ¼ inches long
(Ref: Marcheschi 2008)

viii. White (with black, purple, red and yellow detailing; yellow ears)
1919-22 (according to Marcheschi 2008)
Stamp: 'Amphora, Made in Czecho-Slovakia'
Painted inscription: 'Felix'
11 inches high, 7 ¼ inches long
(Ref: Marcheschi 2008)

10.vi

11. THE LUCKY KNIGHT ERRANT CAT

Registered by Max Emanuel & Company, 41-42 Shoe Lane, London EC, China Manufacturers

Reg date: 12.6.1914, extended on 11.8.1919

Reg no: BT52/629/638312

Reg name: 'Statuette Grotesque'

Charm: 'I will fight your enemies for you and help you conquer your troubles in all that is right'

Casts and glazes:

i. Blue (with green, red and yellow detailing)
Stamps: 'Made in England'; Max Emanuel
Painted signature: 'Louis Wain'
Impressed: 'England'; '638312'
5 ¾ inches high, 3 inches long
(Ref: UK Private Collection)

12. THE LUCKY BLACK CAT

Registered by Max Emanuel & Company, 41-42 Shoe Lane, London EC, China Manufacturers

Reg date: 12.6.1914, extended on 11.8.1919

Reg no: BT52/629/638313

Reg name: 'Statuette Cat'

Charm: 'Hold on to me and fortune will smile on thee'

Casts and glazes:

i. Black (with green, red and white detailing)
Stamps: 'Made in England'; Max Emanuel
Painted signature: 'Louis Wain'
5 ¼ inches high, 3 ¾ inches long
(Ref: UK Private Collection)

13. THE HAPPY JAPPY CAT

Registered by Max Emanuel & Company, 41-42 Shoe Lane, London EC, China Manufacturers

Reg date: 12.6.1914, extended on 11.8.1919

Reg no: BT52/629/638314

Reg name: 'Statuette Cat'

Charm: 'I am a sure cure for the blues'

Casts and glazes:

i. Unspecified colour
   (Ref: Dale 1968, page 113)

ii. Lilac (with green, red and yellow detailing)
    5 ½ inches high
    (Ref: Bonhams 2008, which withdrew this example as a fake)

14.i

14. THE LUCKY BULLY BULLDOG

Registered by Max Emanuel & Company, 41-42 Shoe Lane, London EC, China Manufacturers

Reg date: 12.6.1914

Reg no: BT52/629/638315

Reg name: 'Statuette Bulldog'

Charm: 'Stick to me and I will stick to you'

Casts and glazes:

i Cream (with green, red and yellow detailing)
   Stamps: 'Made in England'; Max Emanuel
   Painted signature: 'Louis Wain'
   3 ¼ inches high, 5 ½ inches long
   (Ref: UK Private Collection)

13.design   13.i   13.ii

15. THE LUCKY SPHINX CAT

Registered by Max Emanuel & Company,
41-42 Shoe Lane, London EC,
China Manufacturers

Reg date: 12.6.1914, extended on
11.8.1919

Reg no: BT52/629/638316

Reg name: 'Statuette Dog'

Charm: 'I bring you good luck take it'

Casts and glazes:

i   Black (with green and yellow detailing)
     Stamps: 'Made in England'; Max Emanuel
     Painted signature: 'Louis Wain'
     4 ¾ inches high, 3 ¼ inches long
     (Ref: UK Private Collection)

16.i

16. THE LUCKY HAW HAW CAT

Registered by Max Emanuel & Company,
41-42 Shoe Lane, London EC,
China Manufacturers

Reg date: 12.6.1914, extended on
11.8.1919

Reg no: BT52/629/638317

Reg name: 'Statuette Cat'

Charm: 'Be like me and you will catch on'

Casts and glazes:

i   Blue head and green body (with red and white detailing)
     Stamps: 'Made in England'; Max Emanuel
     Painted impressed signature: 'Louis Wain'
     Impressed: 'Made in England; 'RG NO 638317'
     5 ¼ inches high, 3 ¼ inches long
     (Ref: Chris Beetles Ltd)

15.i

17. THE LUCKY MASTER CAT

[SMALL]

Registered by Max Emanuel & Company, 41-42 Shoe Lane, London EC, China Manufacturers

Reg date: 12.6.1914, extended on 11.8.1919

Reg no: BT52/629/638318

Reg name: 'Statuette Cat'

Charm: 'Bring your smile with you, for good luck awaits you when you see me'

Casts and glazes:

i   Cream (with green and red detailing)
    Stamps: 'Made in England'; Max Emanuel
    Painted impressed signature: 'Louis Wain'
    Impressed: 'Made in England'
    6 inches high, 3 ½ inches long
    (Ref: Chris Beetles Ltd)

18.i

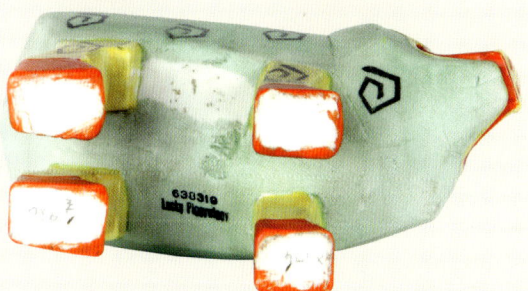

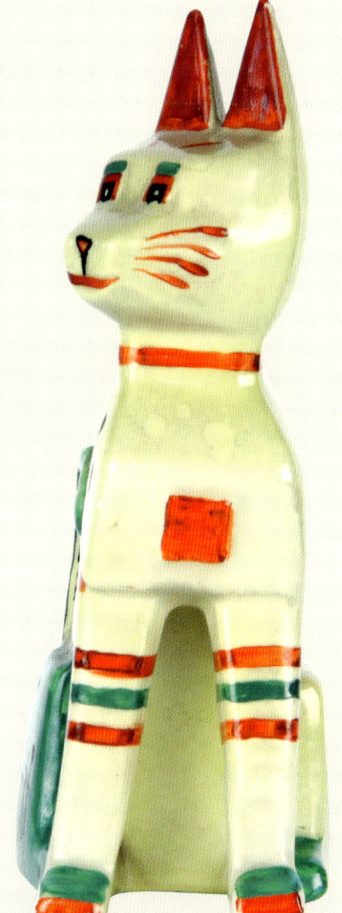

17.i

18. THE LUCKY PIGGYWIGGY

Registered by Max Emanuel & Company, 41-42 Shoe Lane, London EC, China Manufacturers

Reg date: 12.6.1914, extended on 11.8.1919

Reg no: BT52/629/638319

Reg name: 'Statuette Pig'

Casts and glazes:

i   Green (with red and yellow detailing)
    Stamps: 'Louis Wain'; 'Lucky Piggywiggy'; '638319'
    3 ½ inches high, 5 ¼ inches long
    (UK Private Collection)

19.i

19. THE LUCKY PIG
Registered by Max Emanuel & Company,
41-42 Shoe Lane, London EC,
China Manufacturers
Reg date: 12.6.1914, extended on 11.8.1919
Reg no: BT52/629/638320
Reg name: 'Statuette Pig'
Charm: 'I charm all your ills away'
Casts and glazes:
i   Green (with red and yellow detailing)
    Stamp: Max Emanuel
    Painted signature: 'Louis Wain'
    Impressed: 'Made in England'; 'RG NO 638320'
    4 ¾ inches high, 3 ½ inches long
    (UK Private Collection)

20. [THE DRINKING CAT]
Registered by Max Emanuel & Company,
41-42 Shoe Lane, London EC,
China Manufacturers
Reg date: 16.11.1914
Reg no: BT52/673/643807
Reg name: 'China Ashtray'

Casts and glazes:
i.   Red head and green body (with yellow)
     Stamps: 'Made in England'; Max Emanuel
     Painted signature: 'Louis Wain'
     4 ¾ inches high, 4 inches wide
     (Ref: UK Private Collection)
ii. Orange head and body (with yellow)
     Stamp: Made in England
     Painted signature: 'Louis Wain'
     4 ¾ inches high, 4 inches wide
     (Ref: Marcheschi 2008)
iii. Black head and green body (with yellow)
     Stamp: Made in England
     Painted signature: 'Louis Wain'
     4 ¾ inches high, 4 inches wide
     (Ref: Marcheschi 2008)

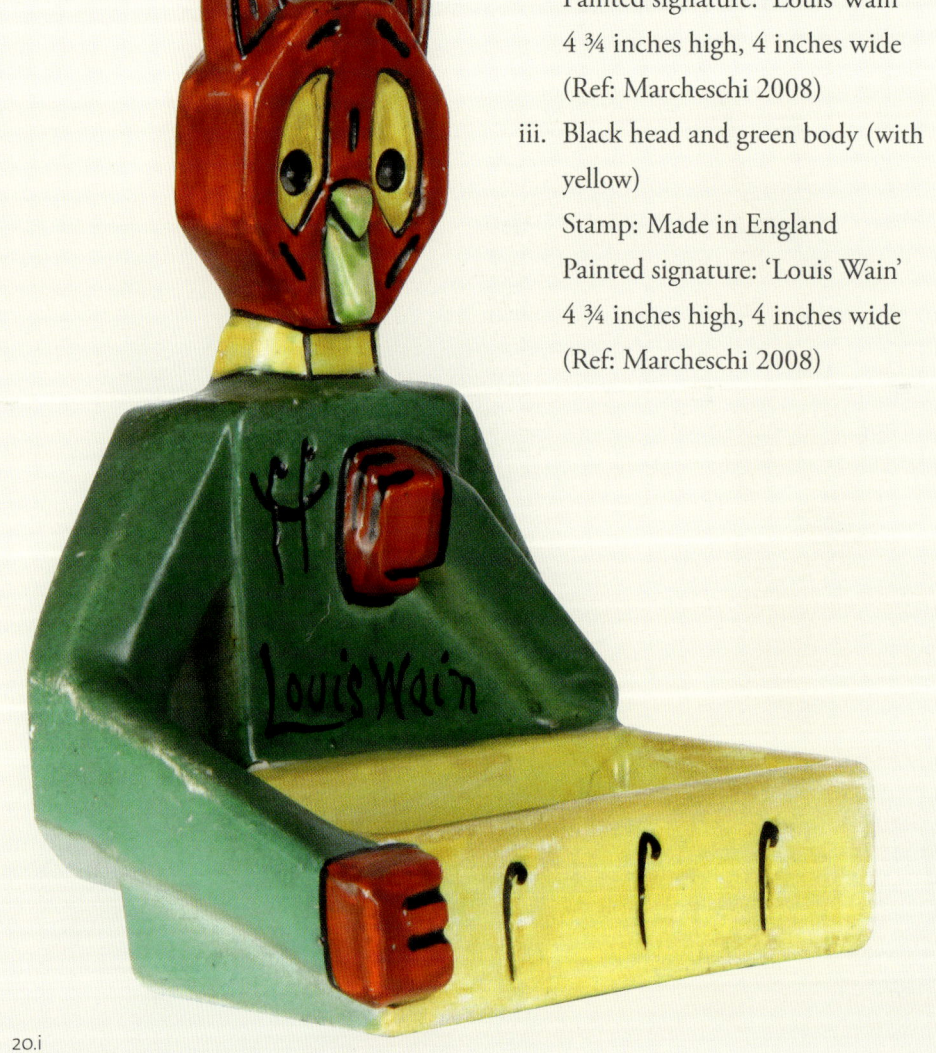

20.i

21.i

21. THE LAUGHING CAT

Registered by Sidney George Parker-Fox,
24 Charlwood Street, Pimlico,
London SW1
Reg date: 10.4.1922

Reg. name: 'The Laughing Cat'
Reg no: BT52/942/689510
Casts and glazes:
i.   Black (with yellow detailing)
      Stamp: 'Royal Staffordshire Pottery

Wilkinson Ltd England'
Impressed signature: 'Louis Wain'
Impressed title: 'The Laughing Cat'
7 ½ inches high, 4 ½ inches long
(Ref: UK Private Collection)

The Life and Times of Louis Wain

Compiled by Chris Beetles & David Wootton
References to Louis Wain and his family are in **bold** type

1859   June: Following the General Election, Queen Victoria recalled Lord Palmerston, leader of the newly founded Liberal Party, to the office of Prime Minister

Saturday 29 October: William Matthew Wain (1825-1880) married Julie Felicie Boiteux (1833-1910) at Spanish Place Chapel, Marylebone, London

William was a travelling salesman for a woollen draper's company, and the son of John Wain of Leek in Staffordshire, a silk manufacturer from whom he became estranged on converting to Roman Catholicism

Julie was the daughter of Louis Antoine Marie Boiteux (1809-1864), a Parisian-born tapestry designer, and Caroline Félicité Josephine Chifflart (1806-1861), an orphan from Dunkirk

Spanish Place Chapel was built in 1791 and traditionally associated with the then nearby Spanish Embassy. It was on a site opposite its successor, the current Roman Catholic church of St James in George Street, just off Marylebone High Street

Marriage Certificate of Wain's Parents

1860   Sunday 5 August: Louis Matthew Wain was born at 39 St John Street, Clerkenwell, London. Through his childhood, he lived variously in the Clerkenwell and Marylebone areas

1861   7 April: The census taken on this date recorded that there were 20.1 million people living in England & Wales

14 December: Death of Albert, Prince Consort to Queen Victoria

Circa 1862   **Eldest sister, Caroline Marie Elizabeth, was born in Islington; birth registered on Monday 3 February 1862**

1862   The Reverend Charles Dodgson (Lewis Carroll) imagined *Alice's Adventures in Wonderland*

Opening of the Marylebone and West London School of Art, Bolsover Street, with Macdonald Clarke as Head Master

Circa 1864   **Second sister, Josephine Felicie Marie, was born in Barnsbury; birth registered on Monday 4 April 1864**

1864   John Wisden published the first edition of *Wisden Cricketers' Almanack*

John Tenniel, *Going Down to the House, Punch*, 10 February 1866

The Naughty Puss, Penny Illustrated Paper, Christmas Number, 1896

Harrison Weir, *Exit Stage Left*, 1865

1865	October: The Liberal Prime Minister, Lord Palmerston, died in office, and was succeeded by The Earl Russell
	Lewis Carroll published *Alice's Adventures in Wonderland*, with illustrations by John Tenniel, chief political cartoonist of *Punch*
1866	June: The Earl of Derby became Conservative Prime Minister
Circa 1867	**Third sister, Marie, was born in Marylebone**
Circa 1868	**Fourth sister, Claire Marie, was born in Marylebone; birth registered on Tuesday 22 December 1868**
1868	February: Benjamin Disraeli succeeded Derby as Conservative Prime Minister; however, he dissolved Parliament as the Conservatives did not have majority, and – in December – the Liberal, William Ewart Gladstone, was elected in his place
	The Académie Julian was established in Paris, at the Passage des Panoramas, and admitted women from the outset
From 1870	**Attended Orchard Street Boys and Infant School, Well Street, South Hackney, under the Head Master, William Pratt**
Circa 1871	**Fifth sister, Julie Felicie Marie, was born in Marylebone; birth registered on Tuesday 4 July 1871**
1871	**Sunday 2 April: The census taken on this date recorded that the population had risen to 22.7 million for England & Wales; also that the Wain family was living at 36 South Street, Marylebone**
	July: The artist, Harrison Weir (1824-1906), organised the first cat show in England, held at the Crystal Palace; he published *Animal Drawing in Pencil* in the same year

Lewis Carroll published *Through the Looking-Glass, and What Alice Found There*

Edward Lear published *Nonsense Songs, Stories, Botany and Alphabets*, which included 'The Owl and the Pussy-Cat'

1872 21 August: Birth of Aubrey Beardsley

1874 February: The Conservative Party won the General Election, and Disraeli began his second ministry

1875 The All England Croquet Club, Wimbledon, set aside one of its lawns for tennis

By 1876 **Attending St Joseph's Academy, 167 Kennington Lane, Kennington, a Roman Catholic school run by the Christian Brothers**

1876 10-12 August: W G Grace made his highest first-class score of 344, for the Marylebone Cricket Club against Kent at Canterbury

1877 The All England Croquet and Tennis Club, Wimbledon, held the first Gentlemen's Singles competition

1877-80 **Studied at West London School of Art**

1880 April: The Liberal Party won the General Election, and Gladstone began his second ministry

23 August: Death of William Thompson (1811-1880), the bare-knuckle prize-fighter known as 'Bendigo'

6 September: The brothers, W G Grace, E M Grace and Fred Grace played alongside each other for England against Australia in the first ever test match in England, which was held at the Oval

Croquet

Who's for Tennis?

How's That, Umpire?

	Wednesday 27 October: Father, William, died in Guy's Hospital; buried in the family grave at St Mary's Roman Catholic Cemetery, Harrow Road, Kensal Green
1880-82	Assistant Master, West London School of Art, at its new premises at 155 Great Titchfield Street, designed by R W Edis
1881	Sunday 3 April: The census taken on this date recorded that he was living at 8 Brook Street, St George Hanover Square, with his mother, four of his sisters (other than Caroline), and three servants. His mother was recorded as the head of the household, and as 'designer in church windows', employing 12 women and two men
	23 April: *Patience, or Bunthorne's Bride*, a satire on the Aesthetic Movement, by W S Gilbert and Arthur Sullivan premiered at the Opera Comique, Strand, and ran for 578 performances
	July: Sold Christmas card designs and drew anonymously for what he called 'minor publications'; took an unfurnished room, but often returned home to sleep
	Saturday 10 December: *The Illustrated Sporting and Dramatic News* [*ISDN*] published the first ascribed drawing to Louis Wain, which he described as 'bullfinches on the laurel bushes', but appeared wrongly titled *Robin's Breakfast*
1882	Employed to contribute illustrations to the *ISDN* by Sir William Ingram, owner of *ISDN* and *The Illustrated London News* [*ILN*]
Circa 1883	Mother was made bankrupt. *The Law Times* of the period gave her address as 8 Brook Street, and recorded that she was a manager and embroiderer
1883	Emily Marie Richardson (1850-1887) became governess to the Wain sisters

A Barrister's Brief

Saturday 20 October: Published his first signed drawing, *Odd Fish at the International Fisheries Exhibition*, in the *ILN*, page 392

Saturday 27 October: Published *Sketches of the Cat Show at the Crystal Palace* in the *ILN*, page 404

1884

Wednesday 30 January: Emily and Louis married at the Roman Catholic chapel, Holly Place, Hampstead, witnessed by Matilda Humphreys and the artist, Herbert Railton (1857-1910)

To Those in Love (detail)

Estranged from the Wain family, Emily and Louis moved in together at 17 Elizabeth Terrace, Belsize Park, South Hampstead

A black and white cat named Peter became the beloved household pet

Emily is revealed to have a cancer of the breast, which was beyond treatment; she became housebound and bedridden

Embarked on long and arduous weekly journeys to sketch and report on dog and agricultural shows around the country for the *ISDN*

Moved to 42 Englands Lane, Hampstead. Emily's sister moved in to help with the nursing

Peter

Took on private commissions as dog portraitist

Spent many hours sketching his cat, Peter, at Emily's bedside

18 October: Published the drawing, *Our Cats: A Domestic History*, in the *ILN*, page 365

1885

Joined the staff of *The Stock-Keeper and Fanciers' Chronicle*, owned by George R Krehl (1856-circa 1904)

She kept on kissing me

Toy Dog Show at the Royal Aquarium and *Crystal Palace Cat Show, The Illustrated London News*, Saturday 30 October, page 451

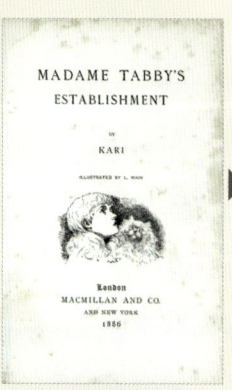

Kari, *Madame Tabby's Establishment*, London: Macmillan & Co, 1886, title page

Harrison Weir, 1889

14 March: *The Mikado, or The Town of Titipu*, by Gilbert and Sullivan premiered at the Savoy Theatre, and ran for 672 performances

June: Gladstone resigned as Prime Minister, as a result of the fall of General Gordon in Khartoum in the Sudan. He was replaced by the Conservative leader, the 3rd Marquess of Salisbury, though he had a minority

1886 February: Gladstone returned to power for his third ministry, but was soon brought down by the Home Rule Bill, which he supported, but which split the Liberal Party. So, in the July the Conservative leader, Lord Salisbury, began his second ministry. Home Rule concerned the right of the Irish to govern themselves within the United Kingdom

Saturday 30 October: Published two half-page drawings, *Toy Dog Show at the Royal Aquarium* and *Crystal Palace Cat Show*, ILN, page 451

December: Given a major commission by Sir William Ingram: *A Kittens' Christmas Party*, a double-page spread for the *ILN* Christmas number. Received acclaim for this, which started his fame as a cat artist

Illustrated *Madame Tabby's Establishment* by Kari (a pseudonym for Caroline Hughes), which was published by Macmillan & Co for the Victorian nursery market

1887 **Sunday 2 January: Emily died**

Moved to rooms at 3 New Cavendish Street, with Peter

Harrison Weir founded the National Cat Club and was its first President and Show Manager until his resignation in 1890

July: First National Cat Club Show was held at the Crystal Palace, London

A Cats' Christmas Dance, Holly Leaves, The Christmas Number of *The Illustrated Sporting and Dramatic News*, December 1890

1888-90   Illustrated regularly for the *ILN* and *ISDN*

1889   **Became a member of the Royal Society of British Artists, and exhibited there for the only time: no 421: *Disturbed* £15.15s**

7 December: *The Gondoliers, or The King of Barataria*, by Gilbert and Sullivan premiered at the Savoy Theatre, and ran for 554 performances

1890   Phil May illustrated W Allison's 'Parson and Painter' for *St Stephen's Review*

December: Produced *A Cats' Christmas Dance* for *Holly Leaves*, the Christmas edition of the *ISDN*

Saturday 27 December: Produced *A Cats' Party* for the *ILN*, page 815, the first appearance of the developed anthropomorphic style of cat picture on a large scale

1891   M H Spielmann, *Henriette Ronner: The Painter of Cat Life and Cat Character* was published by Cassell and Co. Henriette Ronner-Knip (1821-1909) was a popular Dutch artist, specialising in cats

A Cats' Party, The Illustrated London News, Christmas Number, December 1890, page 815

M H Spielmann, *Henriette Ronner: The Painter of Cat Life and Cat Character*, London: Cassell and Co, 1891, front cover

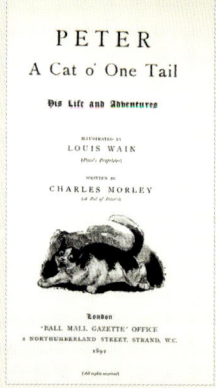

Charles Morley, *A Cat o' One Tail. His Life and Adventures*, London: Pall Mall Gazette, 1892, front cover and title page

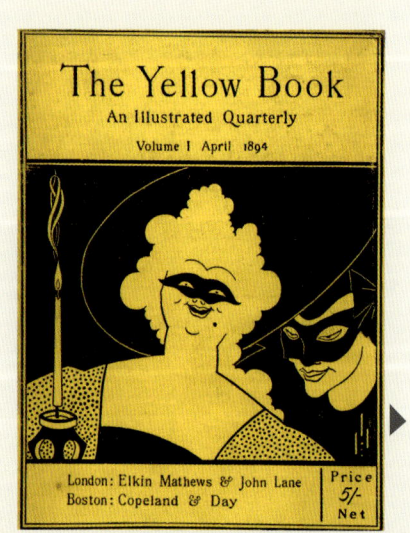

The Yellow Book, Volume I, April 1894, front cover

Sunday 5 April: The census taken on this date recorded that he was living at 117 Park Street, St George Hanover Square, with his mother and his five sisters. His mother was recorded as 'designer in church and art embroidery', Marie as 'Art Embroidress', Claire as 'artist black and white' and Julie as 'artist pen and ink'

1891-96 Served as President of the National Cat Club in succession to Harrison Weir

1892 Illustrated *Peter. A Cat o' One Tail. His Life and Adventures* by Charles Morley, which was published by Pall Mall Gazette

August: Following the General Election in July, Gladstone formed a minority Liberal government and began his fourth ministry

The first *Phil May Annual* appeared

1893 George Newnes founded the Liberal weekly, *The Westminster Budget*, and appointed Charles Morley (1853-1916) as its editor

1894 Full reconciliation with his family effected by Sir William Ingram. Moved with his widowed mother and five sisters to Westgate-on-Sea, Kent, and first settled into 16 Adrian Square

Applied to patent his invention, the 'Steady Cycle'

Aubrey Beardsley and Henry Harland co-founded *The Yellow Book*, Beardsley acting as its Art Editor for the first four issues

March: Gladstone resigned after the House of Lords rejected his reintroduced Home Rule Bill. He was replaced by the 5th Earl of Rosebery as leader of the Liberal Party and Prime Minister

| 1895 | Wain family moved into 7 Collingwood Terrace, Westgate-on-Sea, (now 23 Westgate Bay Avenue). Named the house Bendigo Lodge after the nickname of the pugilist, William Thompson |

Wrote two articles for *The Windsor Magazine*: 'The Duchess of Bedford's Pets: A Visit to Woburn' and 'The Hon Walter Rothschild's Pets: A Visit to Tring Museum'

Applied to patent his invention, the 'New Attachment to Bicycles'

June: Lord Rosebery resigned as Liberal Prime Minister, and was replaced – after a General Election – by the Conservative, Lord Salisbury, who was serving his third ministry

November: Interview with Jas Gordon Richards published in *Chums*: 'A Celebrated Cat Artist. Mr Louis Wain Chats with "Chums"'

Phil May joined the staff of *Punch*

E T Reed, *Phil May*

| 1896-1911 | Served as President of the Committee of the National Cat Club |

| 1896 | January: Interview with Roy Compton published in *The Idler*: 'Canine and Sublime: A Chat with Mr Louis Wain' |

Started illustrating books for very young children, the first being *Comical Customers at the New Stores of Comical Rhymes and Stories*, an anthology published by Ernest Nister, to which various illustrators contributed, including Beatrix Potter, as well as Wain

Became a member of the Committee for the Society for the Protection of Cats and the Cats' Home, Gordon Cottage, King Street, Hammersmith

Louis Wain, circa 1896

Aubrey Beardsley, *The Spotted Dress*, Samuel Foote and Theodore Hook, *Bon Mots*, London: J M Dent, 1894, page 83

Claire Wain, *Yachts at Sea*, 1900

Phil May published *Guttersnipes*

1897   **First appearance of his work in American newspapers owned by William Randolph Hearst**

21 July: The National Gallery of British Art opened on Millbank. It soon became known as the Tate, after its founder, Sir Henry Tate

1898   **March: Death of Peter. 'Died in my hands, a boy kitten again, talking and answering me as of old'**

March: Reconstruction of the National Cat Club with the Duchess of Bedford and Lord Marcus Beresford as Presidents, and Wain still as President of the Committee

16 March: Death of Aubrey Beardsley in Menton

The London Sketch Club was founded: George Haité was first president and Phil May was guiding spirit; founder members included Cecil Aldin, Tom Browne and Dudley Hardy

1899   11 October: Outbreak of the Second Boer War

Wednesday 1 November: National Cat Club produced the first issue of its magazine, *Our Cats*, which runs weekly for 14 years, regularly reporting on Wain's presidency

1900   **October: Exhibited 50 drawings at the NCC show at the Crystal Palace**

1901   **Author of 'The Domestic Cat', a section of C J Cornish (ed), *The Living Animals of the World*, published by Hutchinson**

Illustrated *Cats*, a book of verses by 'Grimalkin', published by Sands & Co

22 January: Queen Victoria died at Osborne House, on the Isle of Wight; she was succeeded by Edward VII

Monday 4 March: Sister, Marie, is certified insane and taken in to East Kent Lunatic Asylum, Chartham Down, Kent

Sunday 31 March: The census taken on this date recorded that he was living at 7 Collingwood Terrace, Westgate-on-Sea, with his mother, four of his sisters (Marie having entered an asylum), and one servant. Claire and Felicie are both described as 'artist drawing sculp'

Rudyard Kipling published *Just So Stories for Little Children*, the longest of which was 'The Cat That Walked by Himself'

The first issue of *Louis Wain's Annual*, edited by Stanhope Sprigg, was published by Anthony Treherne & Co at 1/-

1902

Produced his first work for Raphael Tuck & Sons: the book, *Pa Cats, Ma Cats and their Kittens*, and the postcard series of theatrical cats on the English stage

All Sorts of Comical Cats, verses by Clifton Bingham, London: Ernest Nister

The Louis Wain Nursery Book was published by James Clarke & Co

31 May: End of the Second Boer War, with the result that southern Africa was annexed by the British Empire

Wednesday 11 June: A Grand Concert in Aid of King Edward's Hospital Fund took place at the Royal Albert Hall. Three prizes of £100, £50 and £25 were offered by the Earl of Mar's Coronation March Song Committee, of which Wain was the Honorary Secretary. The first prize was awarded to Miss Alicia Needham

Louis Wain, with three of his sisters and a friend, in the back garden of 7 Collingwood Terrace, Westgate-on-Sea

Stanhope Sprigg (ed), *Louis Wain's Annual*, London: Anthony Treherne & Co, 1901, front cover

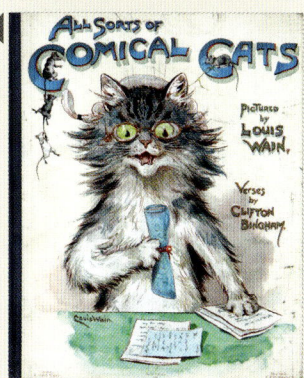

All Sorts of Comical Cats, verses by Clifton Bingham, London: Ernest Nister, 1902, front cover

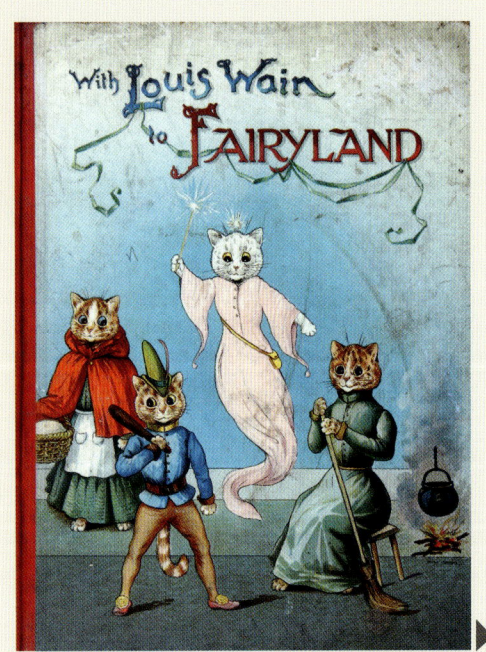

With Louis Wain to Fairyland, described by Nora Chesson, London: Raphael Tuck & Sons, 1903, front cover

Donald McGill,
*Our Tom Cat don't you see
Brought his kittens home to tea*

July: The Conservative Prime Minister, Lord Salisbury, retired and was succeeded by his nephew, Arthur Balfour

5 August: Death of Phil May

9 August: Coronation of Edward VII and Alexandra at Westminster Abbey

Tuesday 14 October: Sent a letter to the *Morning Post*, which was published under the title, 'The Doomed Empire'

***Louis Wain's Annual for 1902* was published by Anthony Treherne & Co**

1903

Illustrated at least 11 books for children, including *With Louis Wain to Fairyland*, described by Nora Chesson and published by Raphael Tuck & Sons

***Louis Wain's Summer Book for 1903*, the first in the series, was published by Hutchinson & Co**

The third issue of *Louis Wain's Annual*, edited by T F G Coates, was published by Hutchinson & Co

17 December: First flight of the Wright Flyer I, with Orville Wright piloting, at Kitty Hawk, North Carolina

1904

***In Animal Land with Louis Wain* was published by S W Partridge & Co**

Donald McGill produced his first comic postcards

8 April: The *Entente cordiale* was signed between the United Kingdom and the French Republic

1905	The fourth issue of *Louis Wain's Annual*, edited by R S Pengelly, was published by P S King & Son
1906	February: Following the General Election, the Liberal leader, Henry Campbell-Bannerman became Prime Minister
	By this year had become a member of the Committee for the Society of Our Dumb Friends' League receiving shelters for stray cats
	Wain family moved into 10 Collingwood Terrace, Westgate-on-Sea (now 29 Westgate Bay Avenue). As before, Wain named the house Bendigo Lodge after the nickname of the pugilist, William Thompson
	The fifth issue of *Louis Wain's Annual* was published by John F Shaw & Co
1907	Summer: Lost a lawsuit
	Saturday 12 October: With little demand for new work in England, accepted an offer from the *New York American*, owned by Hearst Newspapers, and so sailed to New York
	The sixth issue of *Louis Wain's Annual* was published by Bemrose & Sons
	Rudyard Kipling won the Nobel Prize for Literature
1907-11	Sunday 8 December 1907-Sunday 15 January 1911: Published strips in the *New York American* and the Sunday sections of other Hearst newspapers
1908	Wrote regularly to *Our Cats* about American Cat Fancy

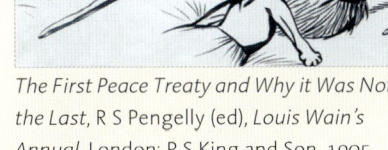

The First Peace Treaty and Why it Was Not the Last, R S Pengelly (ed), *Louis Wain's Annual*, London: P S King and Son, 1905

Louis Wain's Annual, London: Bemrose & Sons, 1907, front cover

Louis Wain, circa 1910

Louis Wain's Annual, London: George Allen & Sons, 1910-11, front cover

April: Sir Henry Campbell-Bannerman resigned as the result of ill health. He was replaced by Henry Herbert Asquith as leader of the Liberal Party and Prime Minister

The seventh issue of *Louis Wain's Annual* was published by Bemrose & Sons

1909   **The eighth issue of *Louis Wain's Annual* (1909-10) was published by George Allen & Sons**

1910   **Wednesday 26 January: Mother died of influenza, and was then buried in Margate Cemetery**

Sailed home from New York

Patented a revolutionary oil lamp, in collaboration with its inventor, but lost the money invested in it

6 May: King Edward VII died at Buckingham Palace; he was succeeded by George V

The ninth issue of *Louis Wain's Annual* (1910-11) was published by George Allen & Sons

1911   22 June: Coronation of King George V and Queen Mary at Westminster Abbey

The tenth issue of *Louis Wain's Annual* (1911-12) was published by John F Shaw & Co

1912   **The eleventh issue of *Louis Wain's Annual* was published by John F Shaw & Co**

1913   **Monday 3 March: Sister, Marie, died in East Kent Lunatic Asylum**

4 June: The suffragette, Emily Davison, threw herself under King George V's horse, Anmer, at the Epsom Derby. She died four days later

The twelfth issue of *Louis Wain's Annual* was published by John F Shaw & Co

1913-14   **Sunday 7 December 1913-Sunday 26 July 1914: The adventures of Billy Kitten, Toby Maltese, Tom Scratch, Tom Catt and The Velvetpaw Family appeared in various American Sunday newspapers**

1914   **20 designs for Lucky Futurist Mascot animals in china are registered by Max Emanuel & Company and gradually put into production in England, Austria and Czechoslovakia**

12 June: The Lucky Futurist Mascot animals were launched at Max Emanuel's showroom at 41-42 Shoe Lane, London EC

28 June: Archduke Franz Ferdinand of Austria and his wife were assassinated in Sarajevo, the event that triggered the First World War, which began on 28 July, when Austria-Hungary declared war on Serbia

4 August: The United Kingdom entered the First World War

Wednesday 7 October: Fell from an omnibus as he was boarding it. Was admitted to St Bartholomew's Hospital suffering from concussion, as reported in *The Times*, and remained there for at least two weeks

The thirteenth issue of *Louis Wain's Annual* was published by John F Shaw & Co

1915   **Autumn: Applied to patent his 'Rangefinder'**

The fourteenth issue of *Louis Wain's Annual* was published by John F Shaw & Co

One of the 'Adventures of Tom Scratch', which appeared in various American Sunday newspapers between 1913 and 1914

The Lucky Futurist Cat and his meow meow notes, 1914

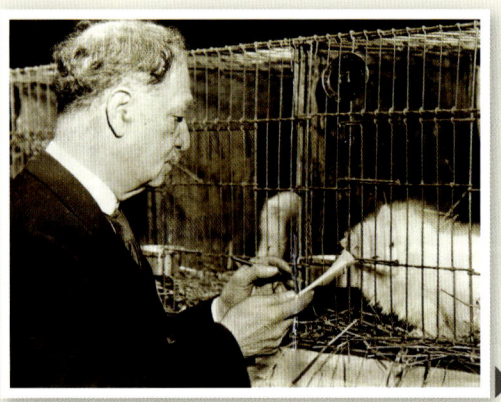

Louis Wain, circa 1917

1916 — **By this year had become a Member of the National Anti-Vivisection Society**

April: Republicans mounted the Easter Rising in Dublin with the aim of ending British rule in Ireland

December: While Asquith remained Leader of the Liberal Party, David Lloyd George replaced him as Prime Minister in order to lead the Wartime Coalition

1917 — **Moved to 41 Brondesbury Road, Kilburn, London, with his four remaining sisters**

8-12 March: The 'February Revolution' took place in the Russian capital of Petrograd, and led to the abdication of Tsar Nicholas II

14 April: Sister, Caroline, died in influenza epidemic

7-8 November: The 'October Revolution' took place in Petrograd

Original theatrical release of the animated films, *The Golfing Cat* and *The Hunter and the Dog*, directed by George Pearson, produced by H D Wood, and written and animated by Wain (with Pussyfoot as the main character in the former)

George Pearson (1875-1973) was a pioneering film director, producer and screenwriter. In his autobiography, *Flashback* (1957), he described H D Wood as the Head of the Rental and Film Sales Department of the Gaumont Company

1918 — 11 November: The signing of the armistice by the Allies and Germany in the Fôret de Compiègne ended the First World War

1919 — 28 June: 44 states signed the Covenant of the League of Nations

14 December: Original theatrical release of *The Adventures of Felix*, the first animated film which names the character Felix the Cat

1920 — Valentine published four new books, with texts by Cecily M Rutley: *The Tale of Little Priscilla Purr*, *The Tale of Naughty Kitty Cat*, *The Tale of Peter Pusskin* and *The Tale of the Tabby Twins*

1921 — Valentine published three 'Rocker' books (shape books with rolling eyes), with texts by Cecily M Rutley: *The Puppy Rocker: Peter Pup*, *The Pussy Rocker: Polly Puss* and *The Teddy Rocker: Naughty Teddy Bear*. However, commissions were dwindling and debts rising, so that his sisters had to work and the mood at home deteriorated

The fifteenth and last issue of *Louis Wain's Annual* was published by Hutchinson & Co

1922 — **Sisters dated this as the start of his deteriorating mental state**

15 November: The Conservative Party won the General Election, and Andrew Bonar Law became Prime Minister

1923 — **Last book – *Louis Wain's Children's Book* – was published by Hutchinson**

May: Andrew Bonar Law resigned as the result of ill health. He was replaced by Stanley Baldwin as leader of the Conservative Party and Prime Minister

1924 — January: Following the 1923 General Election, King George V called on the Labour Party leader, Ramsay MacDonald, to form a minority government, supported by the Liberals

16 June: Certified insane. Admitted to a pauper ward at Springfield Mental Hospital, Glenburnie Road, Tooting, London. Was diagnosed with schizophrenia

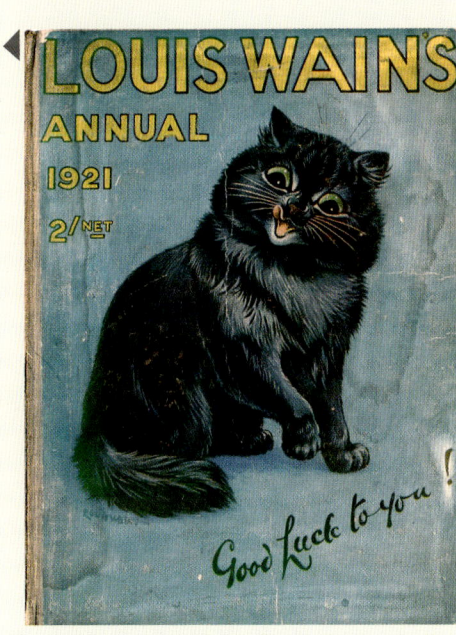

Louis Wain's Annual 1921, front cover

29 October: The Conservative Party won the General Election, and Stanley Baldwin began his second ministry

1925

A typical example of the work produced by Wain at Springfield and Napsbury hospitals

Discovered in Springfield Hospital by Dan Rider, a member of a committee charged with visiting asylums. As a result, Rider set up the Louis Wain Fund, with the aid of Mrs Cecil Chesterton (sister-in-law of G K Chesterton), and the support of influential signatories

Daniel James Rider (born 1869) had a bookshop at 36 St Martin's Court, off the Charing Cross Road, specialising in the Arts, Philosophy and left-wing Politics, with 'books by Fabian writers specially required'. It was a meeting place for writers and artists in the early years of the twentieth century. He was a member of Britain's first socialist political party, the Social Democratic Federation, and founder of the War Rents League, which campaigned for the rights of tenants

Monday 24 August: Through the intervention of Prime Minister, Ramsay MacDonald, Wain was transferred to the Bethlem Royal Hospital, St George's Fields, Southwark

Thursday 27 August: BBC London 2LO broadcast an appeal message written by H G Wells and read by the actor Robert Loraine

Tuesday 8 September: The Fund Committee met and recognised the needs of Wain's sisters. As a result, the £1,500 raised by the Appeal Fund was extended to a new target of £3,000

Sunday 4 October-Saturday 7 November: A selling exhibition was held at XXI Gallery, 3 Durham House Street, Adelphi, London, in aid of the artist. The Louis Wain Fund published *A Souvenir of Louis Wain's Work* in conjunction with it

1926	3-13 May: General Strike, called by the General Council of the Trades Union Congress
1929	**April: The *Daily Mail* announced a further appeal, guaranteed by Ramsay MacDonald, who also agreed a small civil list pension for Wains' three remaining sisters in recognition of their brother's 'services to popular art'**
	30 May: The General Election resulted in a hung parliament, Ramsay MacDonald's Labour Party winning most seats but failing to gain a majority
	October: The Wall Street Crash
1930	**Friday 30 May: Admitted to the Middlesex County Asylum, Napsbury, near St Albans, Hertfordshire, and staying there until his death in 1939**
Circa 1931	**Produced his final postcard series for Raphael Tuck & Sons, 'Louis Wain Mascots'**
1931	**Monday 20 July-Friday 14 August: A selling 'Exhibition of drawings by Louis Wain', in aid of the Louis Wain Fund, in co-operation with Raphael Tuck & Sons, was held at the Brook Street Galleries, 14 Brook Street, New Bond Street**
	Tuesday 27 October: The General Election resulted in a landslide victory for the Conservative Party. However, the Labour Party leader, Ramsay MacDonald, remained in power and led the coalition National Government, which had been formed in response to the Great Depression
1933	30 January: Adolf Hitler was sworn in as Chancellor of Germany

The Contented Mascot, design for the postcard series, 'Louis Wain Mascots', published by Raphael Tuck & Sons, circa 1931

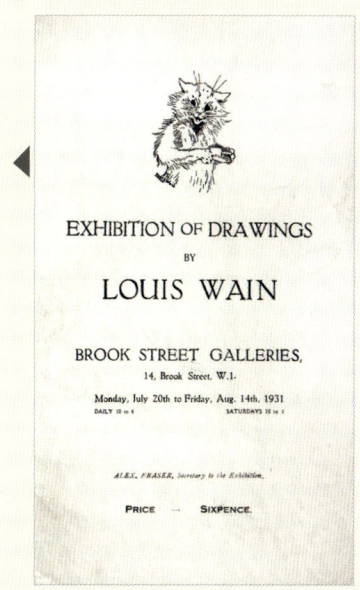

Catalogue to an 'Exhibition of Drawings by Louis Wain', held at the Brook Street Galleries, 1931

Louis Wain's Great Big Midget Book, London: Dean, 1934, front cover

1934	The last book to bear his name, *Louis Wain's Great Big Midget Book*, was published by Dean
1935	14 November: The General Election resulted in a large, though reduced, majority for the National Government, which since June had been led by the Conservative Stanley Baldwin
1936	20 January: King George V died at Sandringham House, Norfolk; he was succeeded by Edward VIII
	Friday 20 November: Suffered a stroke and became bedridden
	11 December: King Edward VIII abdicated so that he could marry Wallis Simpson, an American divorcee; he was succeeded by his brother, George VI
1937	12 May: Coronation of King George VI and Queen Elizabeth at Westminster Abbey
	28 May: Following the resignation of Stanley Baldwin, Neville Chamberlain became Leader of the Conservative Party and Prime Minister
	June: An exhibition of 150 of Louis Wain's works, old and new, was held at Clarendon House, Clifford Street
1938	30 September: Following his meeting with Adolf Hitler, the German Chancellor, in Munich, Neville Chamberlain declared outside 10 Downing Street that, 'I believe it is peace for our time'
1939	**Saturday 14 January: Sister, Josephine, died**
	June: Exhibition at Clarendon House, Clifford Street of 150 Louis Wain pictures

Death Certificate of Louis Wain

Tuesday 4 July: Died at Napsbury of uraemia and senile decay

Wednesday 5 July: Body was taken to the Church of the Sacred Heart, Quex Road, Kilburn

Thursday 6 July: Buried at St Mary's Cemetery, Kensal Green, with his father and sisters, Caroline and Josephine

1 September: Outbreak of Second World War, with the German invasion of Poland

1940	**Thursday 8 February: Sister, Felicie, died**
1945	**Sunday 20 May: Sister, Claire, died**
1968	*Louis Wain. The Man Who Drew Cats* by Rodney Dale was published by William Kimber

1972-73	Wednesday 6 December-Sunday 14 January: The exhibition, 'Louis Wain', was held at the Victoria and Albert Museum. It was curated by Brian Reade, Deputy Keeper, Department of Prints & Drawings
1977	*Catland*, introduced by Rodney Dale, was published by Hutchinson
1978	'Louis Wain. A collection of cats and friends', an auction of 66 lots was held at Sotheby's Belgravia
1983	Saturday 8 October-Sunday 23 October: The exhibition, 'Louis Wain (1860-1939)', comprising 106 works, was held at Chris Beetles Ltd. It was the first of an annual series of commercial shows which continues to the present day, now held each summer
	Louis Wain's Cats, compiled and introduced by Michael Parkin, was published by Thames & Hudson

Rodney Dale, *Louis Wain. The Man Who Drew Cats*, London: William Kimber, 1968, front cover

Poster for the exhibition, 'Louis Wain', held at the Victoria and Albert Museum, 1972-73

Catalogue to the exhibition, 'Louis Wain (1860-1939)', held at Chris Beetles Ltd, 1983

Louis Wain's Cats, compiled and introduced by Michael Parkin, London: Thames & Hudson, 1983, front cover

Catalogue to the exhibition, 'Louis Wain', held at Chris Beetles Ltd, 1989

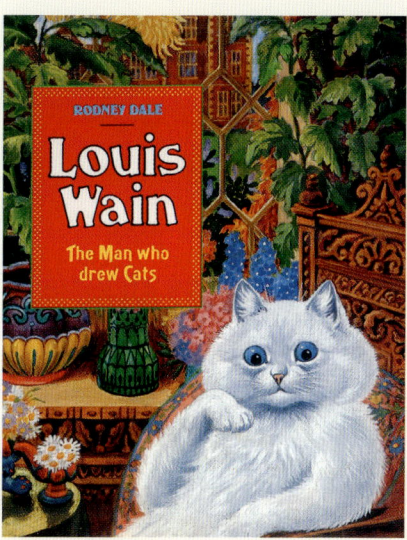
Rodney Dale, *Louis Wain. The Man Who Drew Cats*, London: Chris Beetles Ltd, 2000, front cover

Peter Haining (ed), *A Cat Compendium. The Worlds of Louis Wain*, London: Peter Owen Publishers, 2004, front cover

1986   Saturday 26 July-Saturday 27 September: 'Cats! An exhibition of [133 of] the works of Louis Wain (1860-1939)' was held at York City Art Gallery. The curator was Chris Beetles

1989   5-21 July: The Exhibition, 'Louis Wain', comprising 69 works, was held at Chris Beetles Ltd, to commemorate the 50th anniversary of the artist's death

1991   *Louis Wain. The Man Who Drew Cats* by Rodney Dale appeared in a revised edition with additional colour plates, published by Michael O'Mara Limited in association with Chris Beetles Ltd

2000   *Louis Wain. The Man Who Drew Cats* by Rodney Dale was republished by Chris Beetles Ltd

2004   *A Cat Compendium. The Worlds of Louis Wain*, edited and introduced by Peter Haining, was published by Peter Owen Publishers

Index

Académie Julian 232
Adventures of Felix, The 247
Albert, Prince Consort 231
Aldin, Cecil 240
All England Croquet and Tennis Club, Wimbledon 233
All England Croquet Club, Wimbledon 233
Amphora 208, 210, 213-14, 218-19, 221, 223
Amphora Works Riessner 208
Antiques Roadshow, The 54
anthropomorphic art 29, 82
anti-semitism 117
armistice 246
Asquith, Henry Herbert 115-17, 244, 246
athletics 51
Austria 211, 245
Austria-Hungary 208, 245
avant-garde movement 208

Baldwin, Stanley 247-48, 250
Balfour, Arthur 242
Bamfords 212
BBC London 2L0 248
BBC1 54
Beardsley, Aubrey 233, 238, 240
Bedford, Duchess of 239-40
Beetles, Chris 253 *see also* Chris Beetles Ltd
Bendigo Lodge 17, 51, 65, 239, 243
'Bendigo' *see* Thompson, William
Beresford, Lord Marcus 240
Bethlem Royal Hospital 7, 57, 61, 248; Archive and Museum 152
billiards 21, 122
Bingham, Clifton 241
Birrell, Augustine 114
blogchasenantiques.com 212
Blurb.com 212
boating 13, 124
Boer War, Second 240-41
bohemian world 14, 100, 140
Boiteux, Julie Felicie (Wain) 8, 18, 42-43, 53, 60, 65-66, 230, 234-35, 238-39, 241-42, 244
Bonhams 211, 212
Book of the Cat, The 52
bowling 118
boxing 17, 51
Braque, Georges 208
Browne, Tom 240
Burne-Jones, Edward 32

Campbell-Bannerman, Henry 243-44
card games 124-25
Carroll, Lewis 231-33
Cat Compendium. The Worlds of Louis Wain, A 253
cat diseases 136
Cat Fancy 42, 53, 243
Catland 9, 252
Cats 240
cats (Louis Wain's subjects)
　dining 134-35;
　fashion 14, 40, 126;
　health 136-39;
　law 108-11;
　music 14-15, 100-07, 195;
　politics 112-17;
　sport 7, 12-13, 16-17, 20-21, 118-25, 142-43, 233
cats (Louis Wain's types)
　anthropomorphic 11, 46, 96, 137;
　'dumpty' 40, 144;
　futurist mascot 8, 40, 53-54, 208-29, 245;
　naturalistic 11, 22, 72, 211;
　striped 113, 146
Catsupshire 48
Cattyland 48
Census 231-32, 234, 238, 241
ceramics 6, 8-9, 40, 53-55, 76, 208-29, 245
Chamberlain, Neville 250
charms 8, 210
Chesson, Nora 242
Chesterton, Mrs Cecil 248
Chris Beetles Ltd 212, 252-53 *see also* Beetles, Chris
Chums 239
Church of the Sacred Heart 63, 251
Clanricarde, Lord 114
Clarendon House 250
Clarke, Macdonald 231
Clerkenwell, London 42, 231
Come Birdie Come 52
Compton, Roy 64-70, 239
Cornish, C J 240
cricket 14, 17, 20, 120, 233
croquet 233
Crystal Palace 31, 232, 236, 240
Cubism 208
Czecho-Slovakia 208, 245

Daily Express 209
Daily Graphic 57
Daily Mail 249
Dale, Rodney 9, 39, 64, 101, 210, 212, 251-53
Davies, Dr David 56
Davison, Emily 245
Deakin, Alfred 115

Delulio, Cynthia 141
Deuxberry, Fred 60
Disraeli, Benjamin 232-33
Dodgson, The Reverend Charles *see* Carroll, Lewis
dogs (ceramic) 54, 209, 225-26;
　muzzling of 23
Drinking Cat, The (ceramic) 8, 228

Easter Rising, Dublin 116, 246
Edward VII, King 241-42, 244
Edward VIII, King 250
Edwardian era 6, 9, 13, 31, 96, 118, 126, 140, 149, 208
Emanuel, Max 208-10 *see also* Max Emanuel & Company and Max Emanuel Shoe Lane showroom
Entente cordiale 113, 242
Especially Cats, Louis Wain's Humorous Postcards 141
Every Child's Own Picture Book 40
'Exhibition of Works by the Italian Futurist Painters' 208

fakes (ceramics) 211
Fauvism 208
February Revolution, Russia 246
Felix the Cat 211, 247
fencing 51, 120
Fireside (stamp) 211
fishing 17, 51
football 120, 143
Franz Ferdinand, Archduke of Austria 245
Free Trade 112, 115
Frith, William Powell 7
Futurism 54, 208
Futurist Cat, The (ceramic) 218
futurist cats (ceramics) 6, 8, 40, 53-54, 208-29, 245

Gaumont Company 246
General Strike 249
George V, King 244-45, 247, 250
George VI, King 250
Germany 208, 246, 249
Gilbert and Sullivan 108, 234, 236-37
Gladstone, William Ewart 232-33, 236, 238
golf 13, 17, 20, 46, 123
Golfing Cat, The 246
Gordon, General 236
Grace, W G 233
Grafton Galleries 208
Grimalkin 240
'grotesque' (ceramic) 54
Guttersnipes 240
Guttman-Maclay collection 152

Hackney, London 43, 232
Haining, Peter 253

Haité, George 240
Hammersmith, London 239
Hampstead, London 45, 235
Happy Jappy Cat, The (ceramic) 211, 225
Hardy, Dudley 240
Harland, Henry 238
Hearst, William Randolph 108, 240
Hearst Newspapers 40, 53, 243
Hitler, Adolf 249-50
Hochen, George 212
Home Rule Bill 116, 236, 238
Hughes, Caroline 236
Humphreys, Matilda 235
Hunter and the Dog, The 246

Idler, The 64-70, 83, 118, 239
Illustrated London News, The (ILN) 7, 24, 31, 44-46, 49, 69, 96, 234-37
Illustrated Sporting and Dramatic News, The (ISDN) 44, 68, 234-35, 237
Imperial Amphora, Austria 208
In Animal Land with Louis Wain 242
influenza outbreak 55, 244, 246
Ingram, Collingwood 101
Ingram, Sir Herbert 44
Ingram, Sir William 44-45, 51, 64, 69, 96, 101, 234, 236, 238
Institute of Psychiatry 56
Isaacs, Godfrey 117
Isaacs, Sir Rufus 117

Japonism 208
John F Shaw & Co 96, 243-45

Kari 236
Kennington, London 43, 233
Kensal Green, London 63, 234, 251
Keystone Cops 140
Kilburn, London 55, 63, 246, 251
Kipling, Rudyard 241, 243
Kitty Hawk 242
Ko Ko 108
Krehl, George R 235

Lady's Pictorial 68
Large Cat (ceramic) 214
Laughing Cat, The (ceramic) 229
Laurel and Hardy 140
Law, Andrew Bonar 247
League of Nations 246
Lear, Edward 233
Leek, Staffordshire 42, 230
Lloyd George, David 117, 246
London Sketch Club 240

Loraine, Robert 248
Louis Wain Fund 57, 248-49
Louis Wain Nursery Book, The 241
Louis Wain. Lucky Futurist Mascot Cats 212
Louis Wain. The Man Who Drew Cats 9, 39, 63, 64, 212, 251-53
Louis Wain's Annuals 6, 14, 61, 96-99, 104, 112-17, 126-34, 139-42, 146-47, 241-45, 247
Louis Wain's Children's Book 247
Louis Wain's Great Big Midget Book 62, 250
Louis Wain's Summer Book, 242
Lucky Black Cat, The (ceramic) 8, 224
Lucky Bowl Cat, The (ceramic) 216
Lucky Bully Bulldog, The (ceramic) 209, 225
Lucky Futurist Cat and his meow meow notes, The (ceramic) 211, 220-22, 245
Lucky Futurist Mascots (ceramics) 6, 8, 208-29, 245
Lucky Haw Haw Cat, The (ceramic) 226
Lucky Knight Errant Cat, The (ceramic) 8, 224
Lucky Mascot Cat, The (ceramic) 213
Lucky Master Cat, The (ceramic) 8, 216-17, 222-23, 227
Lucky Pig, The (ceramic) 8, 228
Lucky Piggywiggy, The (ceramic) 227
Lucky Road Hog Cat, The (ceramic) 209, 219
Lucky Sphinx Cat, The (ceramic) 6, 213-14, 226

MacDonald, Ramsay 57, 247-49
Mace, Jem 17, 51, 118
Madame Tabby's Establishment 31, 45, 236
Manx Island 48
Marcheschi, Cork 210-12
Margate 13, 118, 244
Martin, Tracy 212
Marylebone and West London School of Art 231
Marylebone, London 230-33
Max Emanuel & Company 208, 245 *see also* Emanuel, Max
Max Emanuel showroom 53, 209, 245
May, Phil 14, 100-01, 140, 237, 239-40, 242 *see also Phil May Annual*
McCrow, Tiggy 58
McGill, Donald 242
mental hospitals 8, 42, 53 *see also* Bethlem Royal Hospital, Napsbury Hospital and Springfield Mental Hospital, Tooting
Michtom, Morris 209
Middlesex County Asylum *see* Napsbury Hospital
Mitterteich, Bavaria, Germany 208-09
Morley, Charles 238
Morning Post 242
Mosanic Pottery 208-09
Mouseyshire 48
Myra's Threepenny Journal 11

Napsbury Hospital 7, 9-18, 39, 60-62, 248-51
National Anti-Vivisection Society 246
National Cat Club 49, 69, 236, 238-40
National Gallery of British Art 240
National Insurance Bill 117
New York American 243
Newnes, George 238
Nicholas II, Tsar of Russia 246
Nister, Ernest 239, 241
Nobel Prize for Literature 243

O'Connor, Thomas Power 114
October Revolution, Russia 246
Orchard Street Boys and Infant School 43, 232
Our Cats 240, 243

Pall Mall Gazette 238
Palmerston, Lord 230, 232
Parker-Fox, Sidney George 211
Parkin, Michael 252
Patent Office 209
Pearson, George 246
Peter. A Cat o' One Tail. His Life and Adventures 238
Peter the Great (pet cat) 6, 45, 49, 66, 68, 82, 235-36, 240
Phil May Annual see also May, Phil 238
Picasso, Pablo 208
pigs (ceramic) 8, 54, 209, 227-28
Poland, German invasion of 251
postcards 6, 17, 53, 88, 140-51, 210, 241-42, 249
Potter, Beatrix 239
Praga, Alfred 14, 100
Pratt, William 232
Proudlove, Christopher 212
Punch magazine 31, 239
Pussyfoot 246

racing 8, 119
Rago Arts 212
Railton, Herbert 235
Reade, Brian 61, 63, 252
Richards, Jas Gordon 239
Richardson, Emily Marie (Wain's wife) 6, 45, 49, 234-36
Rider, Dan 56-57, 248
Riessner pottery 208
Robinson, William Heath 49
Rockefeller, John D 114
Roman Catholicism 42-43, 63, 230, 233-35
Ronner, Henriette 11, 22, 49, 237
Rosebery, The 5th Earl of 238-39
Ross, Elsa 141
Royal Academy 7
Royal Albert Hall 241
Royal Society of British Artists 237

Royal Sovereign Pencil Co 62
Royal Staffordshire Pottery Wilkinson Ltd 211
Russell, The Earl 232
Rutley, Cecily M 247

Sackville Gallery 208
Salisbury, Lord 236, 239, 242
Sarajevo 245
schizophrenic art 8, 152
School Girl's Annual, The 72-78, 82, 90-92
'Second Post-Impressionist Exhibition' 208
Simpson, Francis 52-53
Simpson, Wallis 250
skating 124
Social Democratic Federation 248
Society for the Protection of Cats 239
Society of Our Dumb Friends' League 243
Sotheby's 252
Souvenir of Louis Wain's Work, A 248
Spanish Place Chapel 230
Speakers' Corner 112
Sprigg, Stanhope 241
Springfield Mental Hospital, Tooting 7, 56, 247-48
St Albans 61, 249
St Bartholomew's Hospital 55, 245
St Joseph's Academy 43, 233
St Mary's Roman Catholic Cemetery 63, 234, 251
Stellmacher & Keppel 208
Stock-Keeper and Fanciers' Chronicle, The 235
swimming 51, 118, 149

Tabbyshire 48
Tales from Catland 31
Tate, Sir Henry 240
Tate Gallery *see* National Gallery of British Art
Teddy Bear 209
tennis 20, 118-19, 233
Thompson, William 'Bendigo' 17, 51, 233, 239, 243
Times, The 55, 63, 245
Tom and Jerry 150
Trades Union Congress 249
tug of war 21
Turn-Teplitz, Bohemia, Austria-Hungary 208
Twenty-one Gallery *see* XXI Gallery

Van Gogh, Vincent 152
Versailles Treaty 211
Victoria, Queen 230-31, 241
Victoria and Albert Museum 8, 63, 252
Victorian era 22, 29, 42, 48, 236

Wain, Caroline 42, 53, 55, 231, 234, 246, 251
Wain, Claire 13, 42, 53, 56, 62-63, 232, 238, 240-41, 251

Wain, Felicie 42, 53, 56, 63, 232, 241, 251
Wain, Josephine 42, 53, 56, 62, 231, 250-51
Wain, Julie Felicie *see* Boiteux, Julie Felicie
Wain, Louis
  ambidexterity 38-39, 60-61;
  America, visit to 40, 53, 55, 108, 117, 208, 243-44;
  athletics 51;
  biographies 9, 63, 100;
  birth 42, 231;
  boxing 15, 17, 118;
  burial 63, 251;
  career development 44;
  cat theories 49-50, 58;
  cat subjects:
    dining 134-35;
    fashion 14, 40, 126;
    health 136-39;
    law 108-11;
    music 14-15, 100-07, 195;
    politics 112-17;
    sport 7, 12-13, 16-17, 20-21, 118-25, 142-43, 233
  cat types:
    anthropomorphic 11, 46, 96, 137;
    'dumpty' 40, 144;
    futurist mascot 8, 40, 53-54, 208-29, 245;
    naturalistic 11, 22, 72, 211;
    striped 113, 146;
    'wallpaper cats' 8, 58, 60-61, 204, 206-07
  ceramics 6, 8-9, 40, 53-55, 76, 208-29, 245;
  character 6, 38-39, 40, 43, 84;
  childhood 42, 67, 231-33;
  collectability 8-9, 140-41, 212;
  death 62, 251;
  debts 53, 247;
  early life and work 6, 22, 31, 36, 42, 64;
  education 43, 67, 100, 232-33;
  exhibitions 8, 53-54, 57, 63, 209, 237, 240, 248-50, 252-53;
  fame 31, 45, 49, 53, 55, 64, 96, 140, 236;
  family 18, 42, 44, 51, 53, 55-56, 65, 230-32, 234-35, 238-39, 241, 243-44, 246, 249-51;
  father *see* Wain, William Matthew;
  fencing 51;
  financial difficulties 6, 53-55, 108, 247;
  first signed drawing 235;
  Futurist cats 6, 8, 40, 53-54, 208-29, 245;
  harelip 42;
  Honorary Secretary, Earl of Mar's Coronation March Song Committee 241;
  hospital decorations 18, 62;
  humour 13, 31, 48, 73, 84, 108, 134, 140;
  illustrated books 31-32, 40, 45, 53, 62, 236, 239, 241-42, 247, 250;

inventions 50, 53, 208, 238-39, 244;
journalism 44-45, 52;
lack of business acumen 32, 36, 39-40, 53-55;
later life and work 7-9, 20-21, 57-63, 152-207;
lawsuit 108, 243;
marriage 45, 235;
mental illness/schizophrenia 7-8, 42, 55-56, 61, 96, 152, 247;
method of drawing 72-78;
mother *see* Boiteux, Julie Felicie;
musical interests 14, 43, 100-07;
observation of animals 90-91;
  on cats 49-50, 58, 90-91;
patents 50, 208-09, 238-39, 244-45;
pets and attitude to animals 6, 42, 45, 49, 58, 66-68, 72-78, 82-84, 90-92, 235-36, 239-40;
political views 112-117;
postcards 6, 17, 53, 88, 140-51, 210, 241, 249;
President, National Cat Club 49, 238, 240;
scarlet fever 42;
schizophrenia 7-8, 56, 61, 152, 247;
scientific theories 49-51;
sporting interests 13, 17, 20-21, 51, 65, 118-25, 136;
suffers stroke 62, 250;
symmetrical drawings 8, 60-61;
teaching career 43-44, 234
Wain, Marie 42, 53, 232, 238, 241, 244
Wain, William Matthew 18, 42, 44, 63, 230, 234, 251
Wall Street Crash 249
War Rents League 248
Weir, Harrison 29, 31, 232, 236, 238
Wells, H G 6, 57, 248
West London School of Art 43, 233-34
Westgate-on-Sea 17, 51, 53, 55, 64-65, 238-39, 241, 243
Westgate-on-Sea Tennis Club 21, 118
White, C A 52
William Kimber 64, 212, 251-52
Windsor Magazine, The 239
Wisden Cricketers' Almanack 231
With Louis Wain to Fairyland 242
Wood, H D 55, 246
wood-engraving 31
Woolwich Arsenal 43
worldcollectorsnet.com 212
World War, First 6, 31, 54, 116, 146, 208, 210, 245-46
World War, Second 251
Wright, Orville 242
writeantiques.com 212

XXI Gallery 248

Yellow Book, The 238
York City Art Gallery 253